OUT OF THESE ASHES

Real-Life Stories
from Mid-Michigan

Published in Beaverton, Oregon, by Good Catch Publishing.
www.goodcatchpublishing.com
V1.1

Printed in the United States of America

Table of Contents

DEDICATION

This book is for all who have been left with the ashes of a broken life. To those who feel that they can no longer live a life controlled by addictions, chained by regret and cheated by past mistakes. To those who feel empty and hopeless. To all who long for a brighter day, may you find hope and transformation in the stories of this book.

ACKNOWLEDGEMENTS

I would like to thank Andy Shaver for his vision for this book and for his hard work in making it a reality. To those who shared their personal stories, thank you for your boldness and vulnerability.

This book would not have been published without the amazing efforts of our project manager and editor, Hayley Pandolph. Her untiring resolve pushed this project forward and turned it into a stunning victory. Thank you for your great fortitude and diligence. Deep thanks to our incredible editor in chief, Michelle Cuthrell, and executive editor, Jen Genovesi, for all the amazing work they do. I would also like to thank our invaluable proofreader, Melody Davis, for the focus and energy she puts into perfecting our words.

Lastly, I want to extend our gratitude to the creative and very talented Ariana Randle, who designed the beautiful cover for *Out of These Ashes: Real-Life Stories from Mid-Michigan.*

Daren Lindley
President and CEO
Good Catch Publishing

The book you are about to read
is a compilation of authentic life stories.
The facts are true, and the events are real.
These storytellers have dealt with crisis, tragedy, abuse
and neglect and have shared their most private moments,
mess-ups and hang-ups in order for others to learn and
grow from them. In order to protect the identities of those
involved in their pasts, the names and details of some
storytellers have been withheld or changed.

INTRODUCTION

What do you do when life spins out of control? When addiction overtakes you or abuse chains you with fear? Is depression escapable? Will relationships ever be healthy again?

Will brokenness always be your companion in this impossible journey called life? Are you destined to dissolve into the darkness of this sorrow? Or will the sunlight of happiness ever return?

Your life really can change. It is possible to become a new person. The seven stories you are about to read prove positively that people right here in Mid-Michigan have stopped dying and started living. Whether you've been beaten by abuse, broken promises, shattered dreams or suffocating addictions, the resounding answer is, "Yes! You can become a new person." The potential to break free from gloom and into a bright future awaits.

Get ready!

Expect inspiration, hope and transformation. As you walk with these real people from right here where we live through the pages of this book, you will not only find riveting accounts of their hardships, you will learn the secrets that brought about their breakthroughs. These people are no longer living in the ashes of yesterday; they are thriving with a sense of mission and purpose TODAY. May these stories inspire you to do the same.

A Dark Road
The Story of Ted
Written by Monty Wheeler

The Afghan sun burned hot, and the city burned hotter. Soon I would know the sights and sounds of a real firefight, and soon I would know death in a way and manner of a soldier. Small arms fire rat-a-tatted on the metal "chicken shield" mounted on my weapon for my protection, and only a fool would fail to duck behind it.

I didn't duck.

My mouth dropped open in disbelief. (This shouldn't be happening to a simple mechanic — those folks hated us, and the bullets they fired were real.) This seemed but one more in a lifetime of fights, but real bullets tinking off metal gave life a whole new perspective.

The last major fight with Mom seemed tame in comparison to the M240 Bravo and its trigger pressing against an uneasy finger.

అఞఞఞ

My life seemed to be about battles. My parents fought. They divorced. They left devastation in their wake. At 13, I initially took my mother's side and resented my father. As Mom found solace and escape in her flights to her favorite neighborhood bar, my feelings toward Mom began to change. I can't say I hated my mom, but many were the bitter words those walls of the subsidized apartment heard, as she fixed herself up for nights at the bar. We kept the apartment from becoming a pigsty, but food always seemed scarce. I resented my mother — I blamed her for being a bad provider and for the lack of food I needed as a growing teenager, but most of all, I resented her never being home, never being "there for us." As resentment built, I found solace in the form of weed and prescription drugs.

Days grew darker, and nights grew longer. Pot and pills gave me that warm and fuzzy feeling I craved. Mom stayed many nights with friends after closing the bar, and she'd wander home the next day to check on us. I felt aimless and useless, without love and without hope. I withdrew more and deeper inside myself, until even the infamous green leaf failed to lift my sagging spirit.

The summer of 2007, nearing my 17th birthday, I thought I'd figured a way out. I'd learned to tune out the sound of the television — it was just noise and only there for a distraction. Nobody really watched it. Mom surfed the net, as I lounged on the old sofa next to her computer desk. She talked about her weekend plans, which like any other since the divorce meant going to her favorite bar. As usual, I wondered what we had to eat in the house. All in all, our typical "family time." Even when Mom was home, she wasn't really home.

In talking about her weekend party plans, she started, "And then I think we'll —"

"I went to see the recruiter today, Mom," I blurted out. Manners in cutting her off didn't factor in — I knew I had to say it or I'd chicken out.

"You what?" She turned to stare at me as if some blast from her past had just entered the room. She looked hard at me for the first time in a long time, and I felt "noticed." Her voice dropped to an ominous tone. "You did what, Ted?"

If I'd not been so self-absorbed, I might have noticed the age in her eyes and stress in her heart, but I pressed on, anxious to get it out. "I went and talked to a recruiter, Mom." I fidgeted under her glare. "I want to join. I want to do something with my life, be somebody."

"You want to get yourself killed is what you want, son. How could you? Berta's son went over there and almost got himself killed. Now you want to? Doesn't matter. You're too young, anyway."

"Mom," I didn't let up, "I want to be somebody, do something with my life, and this is my chance."

Her anger built from something more than just her friend's son. "I said no, Ted. I'm not even discussing it."

"Mom!" My voice raised a few decibels. "I'm gonna be 17, and they'll take me if you'll just sign —"

She swung with the speed of a Wild West gunfighter. Her open hand caught me flat on the side of my face. The resounding smack echoed between my ears. The family pictures on the bland walls danced for long moments. Tears clouded my eyes. "You really are your father's little piece-of-crap son!" Mom screamed at me. "You're just like your father! Your father's son running off somewhere!"

At that moment, I understood my father just a tad more and resented my mother a lot more.

"I'm not signing anything. You're not going anywhere!" she threw in before stomping up the stairs to her bedroom. The one person I most wanted to love me and be there for me had just crushed me.

Not long after that fight with Mom, I was visiting my father and sat alone in my room there. I fetched his pistol and a single round of ammunition. My reasons for existing escaped me. Dragging life out longer seemed impossibly bleak. One never forgets the click of a cocking pistol in a silent room. How deafening can a soft sound be? I stuck the end of the barrel into my mouth. The steel felt cold. I closed my eyes and tightened my finger on the trigger.

Click.

My eyes snapped open. I couldn't believe it. A loud boom should have echoed inside the room and sent me toward whatever waited in "the beyond." Instead, there'd been only the dull click of the hammer on a dead bullet — a misfire. Who could have guessed? My shoulders sagged. It felt like one more failure in a lifetime of failures.

I made a decision. Knowing that, in some way, drugs were at least part of my problem, I determined to get myself clean and off drugs. I moved into my father's house for good. I managed on my own to stay clean, and in 2008, I joined the National Guard.

A Dark Road

❧❧❧

Afghanistan is a world of deserts and mountains, where poppy plants outnumber people, and it's not always clear who's the enemy. In that place, in a world far away from mine, time behaved differently. Minutes were hours, and hours were days. The old fighter pilots on patrol would say, "Hours of boredom and minutes of sheer terror." Bullets flew, and no one knew if he'd live or die. I'd come to this strange place as a simple mechanic, but I found myself behind the chicken shield of a M-ATV, my left hand petting and patting the receiver of the automatic weapon in front of me.

Blocks away to the east of our convoy, small arms fire cracked through the sand-blown city. My squad leader shouted, but I'd already swung to the rear. In a city where the enemy stays hidden, my convoy sat unmoving and vulnerable to sniper fire in front of the governor's mansion. A rescue mission, they'd called it — it felt more like a suicide mission sitting still in that street. I clamped the cigarette butt tighter in my teeth and scanned our rear quadrant for any signs of the enemy.

My daily reality overshadowed my past. If I wanted to see another day, I couldn't live and fight in the past. Nothing mattered except each present moment, and there's nothing like gunfire aimed at you to lower some past squabble on the thought priorities list.

A battered white Toyota came straight at us with the AK-47 blazing out from the passenger's window. The lit cigarette fell from my lips, as I turned my automatic weapon on the Toyota. Rounds tinked off of the chicken shield protecting my torso. Without thought, I answered their AK-47 with one long burst from my M240 Bravo. Bits of the street kicked up in front of the car, climbed up the grill and walked along the hood before shattering the car's windshield. The passenger side gunman flew out of the vehicle and rolled dead in the street. Twenty yards nearer to us, the car swerved hard to the right and plowed into an 8-foot-tall retaining wall where the driver slumped dead over the steering wheel.

I'd killed two men and possibly saved an entire squad. At that moment, it seemed a fair trade. As the convoy growled out of the center of the city, a numbness settled into my bones like the chill of a wintry rain.

Days passed. As the numbness wore off, I began to think of those I'd stolen life from not as terrorists, or the enemy, but as men — men with fathers and mothers, sons and daughters, sisters and brothers, family who would wonder what and how. The guilt of killing began to haunt me. Even though justified and in wartime, the act of killing another human being weighs heavy on a fellow. I wondered why, when turned inward, the gun had misfired, and God had spared me. With nowhere left to turn, in desperation I turned toward God.

For the first time in my life, I turned toward the God I did not understand and began a search for comprehension through reading the Holy Bible.

I am born of Jewish heritage on Mom's side and

Baptist on my father's side, but my mother had not allowed religious training, and she'd never allowed us to attend any churches as children. My knowledge of God and religion amounted to zilch on a scale of nothing to nothing.

With hands soiled by death and a beating heart that shouldn't be, I borrowed a King James Version of the Bible and began my search for meaning in my life. The old style of KJV seemed impossible to understand, but I enjoyed reading in the Book of John. My favorite verse, though, I found in the Book of Psalms. Countless times I read, "Blessed be the LORD my strength, which teacheth my hands to war, and my fingers to fight" (Psalm 144:1 KJV).

I'd been to war and believed myself a "fighting man," so God had to be talking about me. Grasping at straws? Maybe, but even though I would later let go of God for a while, it seems God never let go of me.

☙ ☙ ☙

Home from Afghanistan, I moved back in with my father and stepmother and younger sister. I left God in the Afghan sands and turned to alcohol in the safety of the States. Despite the drinking, I managed to secure a job and find a new girlfriend. Before coming home, I'd broken up with someone, uncertain whether I loved her or whether she was just my connection to home. When I blamed or resented her for something, I "got drunk at her." She served as part of my excuse. I figured I didn't need her or God. I had my new girl, Maggie, a few friends, a little money in my pocket — and alcohol. I abandoned the search for meaning to my life. Drink drowned out the pain of broken relationships and the guilt that still tormented me from killing people.

During one afternoon of fishing with friends, every time Kent or Steven asked, "Ready for a beer?" I'd chug the remains of the one in my hand and go for that fresh cold one. By evening when we gathered to play cards and just hang out, I was plastered. Sometime after switching from beer to whiskey, I passed out on the sofa.

"Hey!" I slurred, as I stirred to life. "I need something for pain. My shoulder's killing me." I'd strained it while on deployment and aggravated it at work lifting more than I should have.

"Nothing here," Steven said. "I don't think there's even any aspirin."

"I'll have to take something, even if I have to go get it." I sat upright on the sofa and dug into my pocket for my keys. "Shoulder's hurting bad. I'm going to the store."

"We're not letting you drive, Ted," Kent said. "Everybody's been drinking a lot, and you're still really drunk." I stared at him but in a sullen silence got to my wobbly feet.

"Kent's right, Ted," Steven chimed in. "You don't need to drive. Just wait a little while and we'll all go."

Anger fueled by whiskey rose to burn my cheeks. It didn't matter that my friends were right and had my best interest in mind. "I'm going whether you like it or not!" I blurted out. "It's none of your business what I do!"

"Don't, Ted," Maggie agreed with the guys. "Just wait for a while."

"You shut up, too!" I shouted at Maggie and started for the door with the keys dangling from my hand.

"Get his keys!" someone shouted. "Don't let him leave!"

Steven snatched my dangling keys and backed away from me. "You're not leaving, Ted. Forget it."

Stopped dead in my tracks, I stared at him. My shoulder throbbed, my head swam and the whiskey tightened the knot in my gut. "Give me my keys!" Each word corresponded to a single step toward Steven. With his back to the wall, we wrestled for the keys hidden behind his back.

"Somebody grab him," Steven pleaded for help.

Kent grabbed me from behind and tried to hold my arms in something like the wrestler's Full Nelson hold. Gutters have no fighting rules. I swung my head back and caught Kent full on the bridge of his nose with a vicious head butt. Maggie screamed as Kent let loose and backed away, holding his nose. As I turned on Kent, Maggie forced herself between us. "Just stop it!" she screamed. "They're your friends, and they just care about you!"

I pushed Maggie harder than I meant to — I'd wanted to get her out of the fray. She stumbled backward, then plopped unceremoniously onto the floor. Anger flew out of me, replaced by concern as I stared at her sitting there.

"Maggie!" I said as I bent and offered a hand to help her up. "Are you okay?" She scooted on her tail away from me. "I'm sorry. I didn't mean …"

"Just shut up, Ted," she said and found her feet. She pushed past me and headed for the door. "Stay away from me! We're done. It's over. I can't deal with you and your drinking anymore."

"Maggie! Wait!" I followed her all the way to her car spewing apologies and promises, all to no avail.

Something snapped in me, and I decided to clean myself up. But unlike before, when I'd given up pot, this time I could not stay sober.

కావావ

"I think I want to try going to church," I told Kelly, my stepmom. We were hanging out in the garage. My dad worked under the hood of our car and listened as I told them about the fight and losing Maggie.

"What makes you think you want to try church?" Kelly asked. She was the most religious figure in my life, although she and my dad weren't attending any church at that time.

"I dunno," I said. "It's just something I want to do, and it might be good for me."

"Well, you've already turned to God once. Why can't you do it again? We can do it. Even if your dad has to work, we'll go. Do you have a particular church in mind you'd like to try?"

"No," I said. "I've not thought that far along."

"That's okay. We'll pick one and go."

The Sunday we chose to go, I sensed something real about God while sitting in that service. I felt no balls of fire, nor saw any burning bushes, but I got a sense of something real. I wanted to know more of God. We didn't go back to that church. Not long after that Sunday, we moved to Charlotte, Michigan, and life went on as before, but I kept thinking about church and God.

☙☙☙

The big fight started when Sarah called me to come get her. "It's late, Sarah, and I'm getting up early. I told you I was hunting in the morning. Can't you just …"

Sarah and I had been dating three months or so. I'd thought of her as perfect for me. We'd met in a sports bar where everyone seemed to be drinking and having a grand ol' time.

"Ted, please, can't you come get me?"

She wasn't slobbering drunk, but I knew she'd had too much. With her, it didn't take much. She'd made the choice to go out with her friends knowing they'd be drinking, and she wanted me to get out of bed and go get her — an imposition. I didn't care that she'd gone out with friends — I wasn't jealous — but waking me up to come get her irritated me to no end.

I got up and went to the rescue. But on and on, I ranted about how stupid she'd been for going if she knew they'd be drinking heavily and the inconvenience of getting me out of bed. Like an old dog with a large bone, I kept worrying it, chewing on it, never putting it down for long.

By the next day, I thought the fight of the night before was over.

"I can't do this anymore, Ted," Sarah said. "You're angry at the world, and I can't handle your temper and drinking any longer."

She had the nerve to confront me about drinking and anger?

"Fine," I retorted in full defense mode. "And remember where we met. You knew I liked to drink when you met me."

"It's not just the drinking, Ted. You're mad at the world. I don't know what to say to you or how to act around you. You're a total jerk almost all the time."

About four days later, her words soaked into my hard head, and I begged the chance to make things right between us.

"I want you to go to church with me," Sarah said.

Not long after moving to Charlotte, my dad and stepmom had found a church they liked and attended regularly. Sarah had attended with them for a few Sundays, but I'd held back.

"The only way we're getting back together is if you agree to go with me. I want to be with you, Ted, but you're going to have to change. Let go of the anger and resentments you're carrying. Let God help."

Then Kelly stepped into the conversation. "It'll do you good, Ted," she said, telling me I'd like Real Life Church. It felt like a last chance. If it would help me and help me keep Sarah, I'd go to church.

Sunday came, and I went to their church. I had no idea what to expect.

The storefront Real Life Church sits on Main Street in the downtown business district. No manicured lawn or lavish decorations. No heavy wooden pews aligned with each other in perfect harmony. Real Life Church has people, real people who welcome you no matter what you look like or where you might come from. What they offered was like a glass of cool water to the lonely one thirsting for something more. They had real smiles and firm handshakes. They walked in the "let's make the new person welcome" attitude.

I can't tell you what sermon Pastor Shaver preached that Sunday morning. I can't tell you what songs they sang or who welcomed me first and last. I can say that something moved me. Something I couldn't see but definitely felt. That Sunday morning I closed my eyes and let it happen. I sat there in God's house and let the warm, fuzzy feeling wrap around me. No drug or drink I ever tried could mimic or come close to that feeling of safety and security, a knowing and believing that something greater than me had control. I had no explanation, but I basked in it, craved more.

After the service, the pastor asked to speak with me. Reluctant and shy, I agreed. He sat in his desk chair, and I stood facing him. He already knew my story — my parents had filled him in about me. Pastor Shaver asked one thing of me. "Would you let me pray for you, Ted? Right here? Right now?"

Nobody had ever asked that before. I didn't know what to say. I nodded, and a warm presence moved in that tiny office. The pastor laid his hand on me, touched my arm. Maybe he thought holding my hand or putting an arm around my shoulder would discomfort me, but I felt the power move through him.

"Lord, Jesus," he began.

I felt my eyes close and my head bow as if pressed downward.

"We know you have work for Ted, a purpose for his life, Lord. We pray that you reach down and touch him. Right now, Lord. Come into his life that he may know you and know your salvation. Open his heart, Lord, so that he asks you into his life as Lord and Savior. We pray in the name of Jesus, Lord, and believe it done. Thank you, Lord. Thank you, Jesus. Thank you."

The pastor's fingers lifted from my arm, and I opened my eyes. The immediate change following that prayer felt subtle but real — and deep.

I stepped a bit higher as I left Real Life Church that morning. During that prayer, I felt like God opened my heart. I asked Jesus to come in and felt my burdens flow out. No wonder I stepped lighter. Three weeks later, on November 11, 2013, the pastor lowered me into the holy waters of baptism. Nothing compared to that feeling, of publicly telling the world of my faith. When Pastor Shaver raised me from the waters, I came up smiling. My baptism was my testimony to the world that our Lord has a book containing the names of all who've come to trust and believe in him. My name has been added to his book.

೭ೂ೭ೂ೭ೂ

I turned to see my wife's smiling face.

I returned Sarah's smile as she blushed. Staying focused on the task at hand became necessary if I wanted to get *anything* done. It'd be so easy to get lost in just knowing Sarah was sitting next to me.

It still amazes me to realize that when I let Jesus enter my life, so much anger exited. Glancing at my wife, I felt her emotion like electricity jumping across the space between us. Life in a bar or in a beer bottle could never compare. I've begun praying that my mother can come to know Jesus as I do. With God's help, I've let go of the resentments against her I held for so long.

For me, there's been no looking back — except to say, "Thank you, Jesus, for lifting me up from the darkness, for taking care of me until I found you."

Fatherless Heart
The Story of Lora
Written by Kelley Leigh

When the contractions started, my 16-year-old body stretched and ached with hot pangs of pain. The biological father lived in another town and a world away. His name would neither appear on the birth certificate nor on a prison sentence for sexual violation of a minor. He would not share this life, which throbbed in me on the verge of birth.

The pending delivery was mine. Alone.

My stepmom drove me to the hospital and left me in the delivery room. She didn't go in. I entered the maternity ward by myself.

Nurses bustled through their medical sequences around me as I rocked and breathed in the cold air of the sterile delivery room. After the pain of the delivery, I held my son for the first time and fell in love with his little round head, teeny fingers and cute face.

Tiny Caleb and I were about to embark on a very long and painful journey.

అఅఅ

My parents avoided the details of my life the same way they chose distance from each other — like magnets of the same polarity, similar but always pushing away. Even as a young child, I had few chances to observe my mom and dad enjoying each other's company. An unplanned pregnancy and quick wedding launched them both into a brief and difficult marriage. They lived alongside each other as passionless roommates without the friendly banter or happiness of lovers. My dad disliked the idea of fathering any more children with my mom. So, when my mom got pregnant again with my little sister, the tepid marriage went cold.

Two years later, my dad's mistress called my mom, and my family permanently unraveled.

The truth blew up in our house sometime in the hours after school and before dinner. I stood in an odd unplanned circle with my mom and dad when their voices started to rise in anger.

"Who is this lady that called me?" my mom questioned my dad as the three of us orbited awkwardly between the living room and kitchen, floating between both, fully present in neither.

"A Cindy called me. Who is this? What's going on?"

"I don't know any 'Cindys.' Do you know any 'Cindys,' Lora?"

I didn't know what to say. I didn't. I was a kid, just hanging out at home after school. I was confused and concerned. After the accusations and denials fell silent, and shortly after this confrontation, my dad drove across town and stayed at a hotel. Eventually, he moved in with Cindy. Dad and Mom divorced. Dad and Cindy married.

Unwanted pregnancies, infidelity and divorce were unspoken patterns passed down and worn like hand-me-down clothing in my family.

෯෯෯

After the divorce, my mom shut down emotionally and struggled to support my sister and me. Looking back years later, I understand that the divorce led to my mom's crippling depression. All I knew then was that after school, my mom didn't really talk to me. She supported us in her own way by working long days at the job she took after my dad left, but she remained distant. She tired easily and disappeared to bed really early most nights. She never did anything special with us and hardly talked to us. It would be years before I would hear her say, "I love you," and that happened only once that I can recall in my entire lifetime. For the rest of my childhood, we lived together and completely apart, in the same universe, on two separate planets.

For a time, my aunt Lila moved in to fill the gaping space caused by my mom's depression. My mom needed help with her daughters, and her sister Lila willingly obliged. She gave generous, unhurried hours to us. She gave us her heart. She carried a kind of internal light about her. Perhaps it was her confidence in God. She introduced my little sister and me to church. In the midst of so much turmoil at home, I felt changed inside. For the first time in my life, I felt overwhelming joy and love. I wanted to go and talk to all my friends about God. We went to church for a little while, but then we moved away and never went back. As quickly as the little flame in my childhood heart lit, it dimmed to almost nothing.

❧❧❧

My mom wanted to move closer to her brother and sister-in-law for help with me and my sister. We moved to a small baseball-and-apple-pie kind of American town — the kind with rows of houses and sidewalks and paved city streets that ambled off into dirt roads and country fields. Neighborhood friends rode bikes outside all day until their moms called them in for dinner.

I slowly gained a couple of close friends at the new school, but I didn't really talk to anybody. I timidly came and went like a shadow. Summer came, and Aunt Lila took us to live at her house so my sister and I wouldn't be home alone all day.

My mom assumed we would be safe with her sister.

But my uncle wasn't safe.

❧❧❧

Rex had a way of leering. Sometimes I could feel him looking at me like he wanted to steal something from me. He stared too long.

One night my aunt Lila happened to notice the uncomfortable tension in the room. She directed her concern at me. "You are getting old enough, young lady. You need to wear different PJs."

Rex protested as though Lila were taking away a toy. "Don't stop it. They're just kids. It doesn't matter." He liked to look at girls. He took pictures of my sister and cousin in their bikinis. And he decided to teach me how to drive.

We practiced driving on long and uninhabited country roads. Rex sat in the passenger's seat, while I clenched the steering wheel and kept my eyes on the road. One day, out of the blue, Rex leaned over and asked a question. Except it wasn't just any question. Rex was leering again.

"Would you ever consider having sex with me?"

I replied like any other pre-teen, grossed out and rolling my eyes. "Noooooo."

"Well, why not?"

"You are my UNCLE."

"That doesn't matter. I have cousins who have sex, and they just use condoms."

I got more serious. "No. I'm not going to do that." An awkward silence settled inside the car as the road passed under the tires and off into the distance.

Back home, I pushed the gear into park and turned off the ignition.

Before Rex lumbered out of the car, he handed me a stern warning. "Don't tell anybody about this."

I avoided Rex for the rest of the summer. When autumn came, my sister and I moved back home with our mom. I mustered up the courage to tell a neighbor about

Rex's car proposition. My statement caused a chain reaction. The neighbor lady told my mom, who in turn told Aunt Lila, who then confronted my uncle.

Rex denied anything ever happened. "I would never do anything like that!"

That was the last word on the matter. Even though my uncle completely repulsed me, in a new way I started to seek more attention from men.

I started to do everything I could to get a boyfriend to love me.

❧ ❧ ❧

"Young lady, you need to go wake up your mom."

Two policemen in uniforms stood in the living room and waited for me to go retrieve my sleeping parent. In the dark bedroom, I leaned over to touch her arm and whisper, "Mom, the police are here. I was out with Sam, and they just brought me home."

She bustled into the living room in her housecoat and pajamas, and the police calmly explained the nature of my wrongdoings.

At 14, my life had become one long series of attempts to get and keep a boyfriend. I was lonely and had learned that I could get attention from guys. I figured out ways to sneak out and be with them. I took advantage of my mom's constant absence. I faked illness and stayed home from school so my boyfriend could come over. Older boys would pick me up, and we would drive around and park and do everything but have sex.

And things even became dangerous.

One night, a shifty schoolmate dropped off my boyfriend at his house and decided to drive me home via an abandoned back road. He pulled over, turned off the car and tried to rape me. "You know you want this," he said as his hands kept trying to touch and grope me.

I struggled from his reach. "Take me home!" I fought him, hit his hand and pushed him away until he stopped trying. He drove me back home in silence. I sat in the car all the way home feeling the same shame and dirty feelings I once felt near Rex.

Even though most boys ended up not talking to me anymore after they got what they wanted, I thirsted for their affection. The time the police brought me home had been no different.

In the living room, my mom shifted her bathrobe, and the police officers explained the details of why they were there. My current boyfriend and I had snuck out and parked on a dark side road out in the country. We were messing around when the flashlight appeared and the officer knocked on the window.

My mom sat quietly when the policemen left. She stared at me with that angry crunched-up face. She rarely mustered herself up to yell very loudly, but her silence was deafening. She grounded me indefinitely and then started back into the familiar silent treatment.

In response, I ran harder to fill the empty space in my soul with men. And I didn't even have to leave the building.

❧❧❧

I was looking for a strong father figure in my life, and he was readily available. The man in the upstairs apartment was 35 years old. I was the 15-year-old girl who babysat for his kids in an ordinary duplex in a small town on a quiet street where people minded their own business and nobody ever asked any questions.

His exhausted night-shift-working wife was my mom's friend. The wife spent a lot of time sleeping or working. She and her husband squabbled and criticized each other a lot. I hung out with him a lot, day after day. No one ever questioned it. Not my mom. Not the wife.

Even though the adults were all friends, I don't remember my mom ever going upstairs to their apartment.

He and I watched a lot of TV and played games, like SkipBo and Uno. He would buy me and my mom occasional gifts, a couple stuffed animals and odds and ends.

At some point, I made it known to him that I would be open to messing around, and one thing led to another.

The symptoms started soon enough. I kept getting sick and nauseous at school, so I rallied up the courage to wander down the hall and visit the school nurse.

"I think you might be pregnant. You need to talk to your mom."

"No way. My mom will kill me."

My mind tumbled in free fall. How would I talk to my

mom about THIS when we didn't even talk about regular, everyday stuff? The nurse saw my concern.

"So, can you write her a note or something?"

That night, I wrote a note and put it under her pillow. When I shuffled into the kitchen the next morning, my mom acknowledged the note matter-of-factly and took me to the doctor. When the pregnancy test turned out positive, Mom informed me, "You have to go live with your dad."

Upstairs, the wife screamed at me and kicked a laundry basket across the room when she found out. Downstairs, I lived in a frozen house full of silent anger. My mom didn't talk to me for two weeks. She did not ask me one question.

The guy upstairs freaked out when I told him. The news of my pregnancy jangled his easygoing demeanor. In the same space where we played fun games and watched TV shows, he became scared and emotionally shaken. He puzzled at how this could happen since we had exercised caution and tried to do everything we could to avoid my getting pregnant. The rest of his words blurred together.

He could have ended up in jail if my parents pressed charges. Which they didn't. In the end, my mom never asked who got me pregnant, and my dad tried to find out, but I would never tell him. So the guy upstairs eventually evaporated from my life, like steam from a boiling pot that scalds the skin before it disappears into the air.

My mom and I avoided each other until she shipped me off to live in a spare bedroom at my dad's house with his wife and their children. I had zero relationship with my dad since the day he left us for Cindy. No matter, my mom wordlessly packed my room into the car and drove me to another town to my new home.

Dad and Cindy lived in a house which always smelled like cigarettes and coffee. I set up my new bedroom and kept it fastidiously clean. I carefully created the big piece of poster board next to my bed and started counting down calendar days until my 18th birthday, until freedom. The wall calendar was my version of a prisoner marking another chicken scratch day on a cell wall. Every day my fingers pushed a marker as it bled another single heavy red "X" on the wall calendar by my bed.

Time moved in slow motion. I felt utterly alone and unloved. Every night the fetus shifted beneath my ribcage, at home inside my tight belly. But the new bedroom at my dad's house still didn't feel like home to me.

౽ఞ౽ఞ౽ఞ

After high school graduation, I took Caleb and moved in with my new boyfriend. I adored Joe because of his strength. And I loved how he was utterly consumed with me. He wanted to be involved in every minute, every second of my life. I thought, *Wow, this guy really loves me!* I got pregnant and gave birth to a second beautiful son.

౽ఞ౽ఞ౽ఞ

"911. What is your emergency?"

"My son isn't breathing! I went in to check on him, and he wasn't moving. He is blue."

When I woke up that morning, I wondered why our infant was still sleeping so long. Baby Joshua developed pneumonia after birth and spent three months in the children's hospital. He had only been home for a week.

The 911 operator kept asking me questions until the paramedics arrived. "Ma'am, what is happening now?"

Joe frantically administered CPR to Joshua's fragile, limp little body as sirens approached in the distance. We followed the ambulance to the hospital, and the doctor immediately informed us that our newborn had died of SIDS. There was nothing they could have done. We needed to hold him one more time, they said, and say our goodbyes.

Friends and family gathered at Joe's mom's house after the funeral. A dozen people stood with plates full of snacks, speaking in whispers and offering condolences. They milled around with well wishes as my mom approached me. Between murmurs and clinking glasses, she moved closer to me. My mom did not cry. I don't remember ever seeing my mom cry. But that day, she inched toward me and said words I had not heard from her since I was very young: "I love you." She actually hugged me. We embraced awkwardly. But in that moment of pain, my mom physically comforted me.

᰾᰾᰾

After the loss of our baby, Joe and I married in a big church wedding. All of our friends were getting married, and we felt pressure to do the same. A lot of years had lapsed since the previous time I'd stood in a church. I remembered the flame I felt as a little girl, but even in the midst of so much celebration, God felt distant. Caleb, then 5 years old, walked down the aisle as the ring bearer. Dressed up in his little suit, he beamed at the prospect of Joe officially becoming his father. But Joe never adopted Caleb.

❧❧❧

For a short time, we were happy. I became pregnant again and gave birth to another son. Mark became Joe's golden child who could do no wrong. Caleb, try as he might, could do no right. Joe constantly berated him. Sometimes Joe would wake Caleb up in the middle of the night and force my groggy son to pick up and put away whatever object Joe deemed out of place. Often, Joe would hit Caleb with a hard smack on the top of his head.

Caleb liked to lean back in his chair at the dining room table. Some nights he'd let his legs dangle as he ate and talked. This behavior irked Joe. Dinner sat warm and ready on that table the night I first wondered if I should leave. Joe walked behind Caleb's teetering chair and kicked the legs. The chair careened out from under my son. His body flailed backward. Caleb's head banged against the wall with a loud crash.

Joe's treatment of Caleb worsened, and his scrutiny of me intensified. I'd arrive home tired after work, and Joe would require a full account of my time. Besides work or errands like grocery shopping, Joe forbade me to leave the house without his permission. He demanded to know my whereabouts or simply went with me, everywhere. He monitored my phone calls and checked tire marks on the driveway. Like frogs in a pot, I somehow missed recognizing the danger in that slow increase of heat in those boiling years of fear.

෴෴෴

Joe found the note when he opened the refrigerator. Earlier that morning, Caleb had carefully taped a piece of paper to Joe's lunch. After shutting the refrigerator door, Caleb left for another day at middle school. The handwritten message was a suicide note. Caleb wanted to die, and he wanted his abuser to know it.

Joe called me at work, and I rushed to my car, frantic to pick up Caleb at school. I was scared and desperate for my son. When we arrived back at home, I told him to go to his room so I could figure things out. But I had no clue how to begin figuring this out.

After the suicide scare, I believe my husband was genuinely afraid for my son, but I saw no signs of remorse for his behavior. Joe did not admit to doing anything wrong. The berating subsided for a while but returned little by little, comment by comment.

I dreaded going home after work. I hated being there. The same deep hole in my soul started itching to be filled by a man who would really love me.

Here and there, at work, among friends, I sought out the affection and acceptance of other men to fill an aching void. Joe suspected my affairs, and his jealousy went wild. Sometimes he would apologize for his angry eruptions, but he always refused counseling. Our house felt like a dangerous boiling cauldron.

Some friends sensed our crisis and invited us to their church. When I went, I felt something I had not felt in years. I felt so hopeless and hurting and desperate, but I started to seek God in my heart. I saw glimmers of hope among the people at church, and that gave me courage for what came next.

ॐॐॐ

I received some unexpected buy-out money from work and used it to purchase a safe place to live. Joe did whatever he could to stop my departure.

He burst through the door and pushed me up against the wall with his fingers in my face. I recorded his threatening phone calls as evidence for the police, but I never received a restraining order.

ॐॐॐ

After the divorce, I returned to familiar ways of seeking love. I dated guys who only wanted one thing — alcohol and physical affection. My body felt empty. My heart felt used up. My soul felt broken, unloved, used.

One morning, after a night of drinking, I dragged myself out of bed and turned on the shower. As the clean water flowed over me, I pleaded with God.

"Please send me a man who will love me!"

I found a new job and new friends. In the freedom that came with a blank-slate beginning, I mustered the courage to confide in one of my co-workers. As she listened, my new friend hatched a matchmaker's plan, and I reluctantly agreed to meet her recently divorced neighbor.

Travis and I went to a Christmas work party and immediately hit it off. Travis was 100 percent different than anybody I ever dated or loved. Gentle with his words, his touch soft and safe, he swept me off balance and enthralled me. We dated for a while before I realized: God had answered my desperate shower prayer.

For my birthday, Travis took me to Disney World. And under a perfectly clear blue sky next to Cinderella's castle, he bent down on his knee. Ring in his pocket, he quietly asked, "Will you marry me, Lora?"

Travis and I married in a church wedding. Caleb walked me down the aisle and gave me away to the man I believe God gave me as a gift. But one thing was still missing in my life.

I found it on the highway a few months later.

❧❧❧

I shared custody of Mark with his father. So every week, Mark and I took a long drive to a midpoint meeting spot with Joe. On my trips alone, I tuned in to various pastors on the radio for encouragement and inspiration. On this particular night, my headlights pierced through a dark night as my SUV zipped down the highway. As mile markers sped by, I listened to a pastor's clear voice. His message spilled into the car like a hundred other sermons before — except those particular words on that particular night struck deep in my heart.

My heart had grasped new hope. My life had felt illuminated little by little. But that night, listening to those words, I knew it was time.

I wanted to reignite the spark that started so many years ago in my heart as a little girl. I wanted to return to the Jesus I knew before I started running after the affection of men. Before I learned that fathers cheat and leave. Before my mom's emotional absence. Before the attention from married men. Before the death of my baby and the cruelty toward my son. Before I became so lost.

I felt a burning desire to turn my life around and finally commit my life to Jesus. My heart started pounding. I felt like my eyes were opening for the first time to something more. In my heart, I knew I needed to turn my life around. There in my chilly car, I felt the ember turning to flame inside of me. My eyes filled with hot tears of gratitude and joy.

The radio pastor spoke an invitation to say a prayer for new life, and I repeated the words out loud.

"Lord Jesus, I know I am a sinner, and I ask for your forgiveness. I believe you died for my sins and rose from the dead. I trust and follow you as my Lord and Savior. Guide my life, and help me do your will. In your name, amen."

I finally recognized how God was with me the whole time, even when I felt alone. I saw that he was there, in all of it. He preserved me through it all. I had spent my whole life looking for someone to love me. Suddenly it was clear. I didn't need to fill the hole in my soul anymore.

I once felt hopeless, despondent, unloved, fatherless.

But after recognizing God as the ultimate good man who loves me, my days started to fly at the speed of light. In the time since that drive in the car, I've grown so much. I've made new friends, people who support God's place in my life. Many of them also worship with me at Real Life Church.

There's a line in the Bible that particularly encourages me. It's in 2 Corinthians, chapter 4, verses 16-18. It reads: "Even though on the outside it often looks like things are falling apart on us, on the inside, where God is making new life, not a day goes by without his unfolding grace."

For a while there, everything certainly looked like it was falling apart. But with God, I am making a new life.

I am at peace on the inside.

And my heart is filled with the love of a true Father.

Living a Lie
The Story of Nicklaus
Written by Ameerah Collins

How will I get her back? How will she trust me again? Why would she even want to?

"I don't know what to do." I shifted in the plush chair and ran a hand through my hair. "Sometimes I lay awake at night and this overwhelming feeling just bombards me with a need to — *to do what I do*. It just comes out of nowhere, and I can't shake it."

Dr. Winchester nodded and jotted notes on the pad situated on his lap. He tapped his pen against his rocking knee and eyed me. "There is always a trigger, Nicklaus — a warning sign."

"I love my wife," I continued. "I love the future we're supposed to build together. The children we're meant to bring into the world. But, how do I not have these feelings? How do I not be this double person with this secret life?"

"Has living a lie ever been easy, Nicklaus? Haven't you had to work hard and diligently at pretending to be the husband your wife deserves? Has it ever been a cakewalk for you?"

I sighed. "No, not exactly."

"And there it is." Dr. Winchester adjusted his black-rimmed glasses on the bridge of his nose and smiled softly.

"There is no magic wand that can poof all your problems away. It doesn't work like that. This won't be easy, so don't think it will. Breaking this habit will be a struggle."

"How long will I struggle? How long will it take to repair the damage I've caused my marriage? To get rid of this …" I picked at my slacks, "this side of me that I hate?"

"As long as it takes, Nicklaus. Like I said, it won't be an overnight journey, but if you're dedicated …"

I want to leave it all behind. Overcome my past. Be the husband my wife deserves.

I just don't know if I can.

જીજીજી

During my youngest years, my parents' marriage was in a state of constant flux. Together one day, separated the next. Dad had a tendency to treat Mom like a trash bag — somewhere he could chuck all his dirty words and even push around a bit. And Mom, she was white, and her family disowned her for marrying my father, a black military man. Without that familial support, she crumbled under his command.

I often wondered why he handled Mom with disdain, yet he treated me and my siblings, Ingrid and Logan, with the sort of love he, being a hardened man, stood capable of showing.

I remember his unfaithfulness to my mother. Growing up, we had random half-brothers and half-sisters due to my father's infidelity. Still, I not once felt unloved. I just felt misplaced. I didn't see myself clearly, and I didn't know what or who I should be. I had no secure belief in myself as a young boy.

That grew even more when Mom chose to leave Dad. I didn't fault her for the divorce. I understood her reasoning. Over the years, my siblings and I saw less of my father and his family and began seeing my mother's side of the family more often. After leaving him, I believe Mom reconciled with her family.

Later, Mom married J.J. I had a bit of a problem with him. He wasn't a bad guy. I'd just become accustomed to being the oldest male in the house, and I didn't want him to steal my role. When Dad stopped coming around, I cared for and protected Ingrid and Logan just like a father would. I didn't want another man to step in and do that. It took a while for me to realize J.J. wasn't trying to replace me, he just wanted to be part of my family.

My real problems started at 11 years old. Being a chubby kid, I wished my birth father had stayed in my life long enough to teach me to have confidence in myself and not always compare myself to other boys. I wanted him to come over and throw a baseball around with me. I wanted him to tell me it was okay to be a hefty kid, and if I'd wanted to shed pounds, then I wished he would have helped me. He was absent, so I turned to other things.

We had a family function at my uncle's house, and I found a *Playboy* magazine in his bathroom. I leaned against the porcelain sink and flipped through the thin pages. I'd never seen anything pornographic or risqué before slipping my eyes over those pages. The photos sort of fascinated me, but they didn't hold my interest for long.

"Okay." I shrugged as I stared at the provocative women. "This doesn't really faze me. They look good, but whatever." I chucked the magazine back in the bin beside the sink and walked back to the family gathering.

The *Playboy* magazine didn't intrigue me, but when I went to another uncle's house, I found a *Muscle & Fitness* magazine in his den. Again, I flipped through the pages, but my interest for the guy magazines piqued. Poking my pudgy gut, I longed to look like the body builders featured in the magazine.

"I want to be them. How can I look like them? I don't even know where to start."

Every time I visited my uncle's house, I darted toward the *Muscle & Fitness* magazines and combed through them. After a few months, I went from admiring the body builders to ogling them. Part of me believed I just liked looking at them, but another part knew I was slowly developing a romantic attraction toward them.

I just didn't want to believe it.

რრრ

At about 13 years old, my family moved to a rural town where everyone knew everyone. The town proved to be a bit of an adjustment for me. It only had one stoplight, which worked during the first hour of private school and the last hour. The school consisted of three rooms: one for elementary, another for middle school and the last for high school. We didn't have extracurricular activities to get involved in, so I never got a chance to learn sports or become as physically active as I desired. Instead, I excelled academically and musically.

I'm not an athlete, I typically told myself. *Music is a good release for me. School is something that comes easy. I'll just be the smart music guy.*

When I turned 16, the private school I attended closed down, and my parents sent me to a public school. Everything was different there. While the high school was comprised mostly of Hispanic people, I was the "token black kid." The school had a music program, drama club, sports and other activities. Finally, I saw a chance to become something other than just the smart, musically inclined kid. I soon discovered my knack for business, graphic design and a more creative side that I'd never known I possessed.

My mom and stepdad took us to church regularly and made sure we knew the importance of having a relationship with God. They stressed communicating with God through prayer and simply staying in tune with him. Ingrid, Logan and I were used to going to church with our mother as small children, but as we grew older we appreciated its teachings more. Plus, J.J. and Mom were leaders in the church and were regarded with much respect. My stepdad served the church as a deacon, someone who assisted the preachers and ministers.

Though my parents kept us in church and instilled

morals in us, I continued to deal with my self-image issues. I also noticed that I didn't look at any of my female classmates and think, *Oh, she's cute. I'd really like to date her.* I had a tendency to look at the upperclassmen, particularly the male athletes, with something a bit more than admiration. I told myself I just wanted to be like them. I could not admit to myself that I was drawn to their outward appearance. I didn't tell anyone about my romantic attraction to the same sex.

I bottled it up and never let my secrets slip out.

Over time, I built a close friendship with another church leader's son, Jace. Like me, Jace didn't have much experience with girls. Although we knew right from wrong, every three or four months we'd get together and watch pornographic videos. As sons of respected leaders in the church, we knew opening our minds up to such graphic sexual images would cause us to want to engage in premarital sex, but we did it, anyway.

But something about the short films stumped me. Instead of focusing on the girls in the videos, my eyes zeroed in on the fellas. I didn't understand why I was feeling that way toward men. I didn't get how I could be attracted to them, when "normal boys" were supposed to be attracted to the women in the films. I didn't talk to my parents or anyone else about my feelings. I figured I'd just deal with them on my own.

One time Jace and I got together and watched a film, but something happened during it. We started to fall asleep while watching it, but instead of drifting off to

56

sleep, we eased toward one another and decided to experiment. It was my first sexual experiment. Our physical interactions happened two or three more times, and I knew we shouldn't have done it.

We decided to keep it quiet. I acted like it never occurred. I continued my involvement in church as the main music guy. I took girls to senior prom, homecoming, winter formals and all the other things I felt like a typical high school boy was expected to do. I didn't want anyone knowing about the feelings I was struggling with inside.

Just do what you're supposed to do, Nick, I told myself. *No one will ever know.*

ॐॐॐ

Going to college, I persuaded my parents to let me live on campus.

"You're still active on the music team at church," Mom told me in the living room one day. "Your stepfather and I expect you to come home every Sunday and go to church, Nicklaus."

"That's fine," I told her. "That's not a problem. I'll be here."

"And you can't live in the co-ed dorms." Mom shook her head. "That's completely out. You're staying in the boy's dorm, so you don't slip up and become distracted with college girls."

Mom still had no idea of the gay feelings I was fighting on the inside. If she had known, she probably would have wanted me to stay in the co-ed dorms. To her, I was just the classic straight gentleman with his head on straight.

Yeah, right, I thought. *If Mom only knew how great of an actor I am.*

In college, I was determined to figure out who I was as a person. I wanted to know if the homosexual feelings were part of me or just a phase. My church never really bashed homosexuality or spoke heavily against it, but my understanding was that the Bible opposed it. Still, I'd been wrapped up in the church for so long, I wanted to try my own path and live a little.

My first semester of college, I rushed a fraternity. Except for Jace, I'd never had a strong friendship with a dude my age. I wanted to connect with and possibly open up to someone about my worries. I couldn't talk with my birth father, because he was no longer around. I was close to J.J., but it just wasn't the same. And my little brother Logan was too young for me to confide in. I figured the only way I would obtain that camaraderie would be to join a brotherhood.

Pledging a fraternity was draining. I always had functions to attend, deeds to perform for my big brothers and I never got enough sleep. My grades suffered from all the wild parties I attended and all the energy I placed into being the macho guy I wanted to be.

The parties and fraternity weren't the only activities taking up my time. I began overanalyzing my life. I had a roommate who constantly had sex with his girlfriend in the bed across from mine. I considered their open actions super creepy, but I kept wondering if I should be more like him. *Maybe I should sneak girls into my dorm and fool around with them.* I couldn't do it, though. I wasn't attracted to the girls in college. Just the guys.

Soon, I became friends with Marcos. He was a boy I physically lusted after, and I guess he had gay feelings, too, because we eventually became sexually active. Within months of trying to "find myself," I quit overanalyzing my internal emotions, abandoned trying to figure out my ongoing sexual orientation crisis and just jumped into the relationship with Marcos.

We weren't the standard couple, though. We didn't go out on dinner dates, hit the movies, have a wonderful time and conclude the evening with some pillow talk. Our relationship was purely physical and, for me, based on lust. Even when I was with Marcos, I felt like something deep within me told me it wasn't the right thing to do. However, I figured, *Oh, well. I can't fix or control my feelings. I might as well conform to them. I'll try this lifestyle, and see what happens. No one will know.*

Marcos became my dirty little secret. My frat brothers had no idea I had a secret boyfriend — I was the reliable party animal they had fun with. On Sunday mornings I reverted into the good churchgoing boy for my parents. And with Marcos, I became his lover.

After a while, living in three different worlds got the better of me. Guilt worked on my conscience, and I found myself telling lies to deal with the different lives I was living.

"You're coming home for church this weekend, right, son?" Mom asked over the phone.

I clenched the phone. "Not this Sunday. I have … college stuff to do."

"Oh, yeah?" Her voice sounded curious. "What kind of college stuff?"

"I just have to work this fraternity function. Plus, I have a major exam coming up. I'm probably going to pull an all-nighter at the library."

"Oh, that's too bad, honey." Mom tried to comfort me. "Maybe next week?"

"For sure." I rolled my eyes at my lies. "Next week is good."

The following week came quickly, and I offered my mother another lie.

"I have to meet with my residential advisor. I can't get out of it."

"Hmm, okay, Nicklaus. I'll tell everyone at church you said hello."

I was so ashamed of my college lifestyle that I didn't want to show my face at church. I tried to make it home every two or three weeks so my parents didn't become suspicious or realize my deception, but it was hard walking into church knowing all the crap I was doing on campus. The drinking, partying, lying to my parents, sleeping with Marcos and trying to keep my frat brothers in the dark about my gay relationship exhausted me.

Who knew living a lie was such a challenging task to maintain?

The summer after freshman year, I'd delved into so many wild and carnal activities, I decided not to return home. I already pictured God seeing my every move. I didn't want my parents to look at me and see through my falsehood. So I told my parents I'd found a job and a couple college friends to room with over the summer, and surprisingly, they had no qualms with it.

From their perspective, I was still their "good boy." My stepdad had gotten a new job, which required them to move an hour away from my college, and my parents believed I was old enough that they didn't have to keep such close tabs on me.

As summer passed, I became weary of my conflicting behaviors. It felt wrong. I wanted to have that sacred "bromance" with my wild and crazy frat brothers. I wanted to continue living out my gay fantasies with Marcos. And I wanted to be the gifted music guy at church. I couldn't have all three, though. Such a disparity filled me with unhappiness, and depression seeped in.

"Mom." I sat on my bed and nestled the phone between my shoulder and ear. "I've been having these emotions that have been just driving me up a wall. I don't feel like myself anymore. I feel alone — like an outsider. I don't fit in."

"Oh, Nicklaus." Mom sighed. "I know we've moved, but you don't have to feel alone. Not when you have God with you. Have you been talking to God and reading your Bible?"

"No." I rubbed my eyes. "I haven't been doing that."

"Son, you know the importance of prayer and maintaining a relationship with God. You know who you need to turn to in times like these."

"I mean, yeah, but," I huffed and flopped against my mattress, "to be honest, I've been going out with my frat brothers and trying to take my mind off of everything. I haven't thought to pray about it."

How can I? I wanted to shout. *How can I go to God when I'm living such a shabby life?*

"I understand." I could picture her nodding. "But going out won't take away the loneliness, Nicklaus. Drinking with your fraternity brothers, going to parties or whatever it is you're up to won't take away the pain you're feeling. I know you've always craved a close friend, and it's obvious you're not getting that from your fraternity like you expected."

"Right. I'm not."

"That's because you know the truth. You can seek acceptance and fulfillment in friends, alcohol and parties all you want, but you'll never receive true acceptance and fulfillment from those things. God is your number one, Nicklaus. Stop trying to replace him."

I groaned. "I'm not trying to replace him. I'm just trying to find myself."

I strained in my explanation. I couldn't really tell Mom that it wasn't only the parties driving a wedge between God and me. I couldn't expound on the homosexual lifestyle I was living. I couldn't confide in her about all the lies I'd told her in order to skip church.

"Don't get frustrated, Nicklaus. I'm just being truthful with you," Mom soothed. "You're feeling this way because you're far away from God. You may not realize it, but you've shut him out. Shutting God out allows negativity to sink in. You can't live a raucous life on campus, then go to church on Sunday like everything is copacetic. You have to be a Christian because you want to."

"I *do* want to."

"Perhaps, Nicklaus. But it sounds like you're living in two different worlds. You need to decide what world you want to live in. The wild lifestyle or the Christian lifestyle."

After I hung up with Mom, I thought about when my mom and birth father were together, and though their marriage was pretty messed up, they still took us to church and instilled their moral values in us. I pictured myself at age 5 walking to a platform and lifting my hands to give my life to Christ. I didn't know what it meant to live for God, I just knew I had a strong desire to give my life over to Jesus — to put my life in the hands of the Lord.

My relationship with God is so off track. I'm not even as close to God as I was at 5 years old. Mom is right about everything, but I don't just have two worlds to choose from. I have three. I can't handle them all. I have to say goodbye to my partying life, homosexual life or Christian life.

Growing up, I never grasped that one day I would have to answer to God for myself. I just thought, *J.J. is a deacon. Mom is a respected lady at church. My folks are good with God, so I know I'm good with him, too.* My parents couldn't save me from my recklessness, though. I couldn't just go to heaven when I died because *they* loved God. I knew I had to make a choice on which life I wanted to live.

For a week, I prayed and read my Bible. It proved difficult for me to break away from the multiple lives I'd become accustomed to living. Even though I'd started spending more time with God, I knew I'd never get as close to God as I desired if I stayed in that wild environment. I needed to break away from the college parties. And from Marcos.

I chose God.

"I can't be here anymore," I told Mom over the phone. "This environment, it's too much for me. I'm not myself. I'm not who God wants me to be. I just need —"

"Come home, Nicklaus." Mom's soft voice quieted my anxious one.

I froze. "Are you sure, Mom?"

"Yes. Come home."

෧෧෧

After I moved back home, I got a job waiting tables. I went back to church and threw myself into creating a great church choir. Though I desired to renew my relationship with God and completely dedicate my life to Jesus, I still battled my homosexual feelings. They were much stronger than the emotions I experienced before college. Since I'd given into those sexual feelings in college, my ache for what I experienced with Marcos was more intense. I no longer solely felt an attraction to men, I *yearned* for some sort of sexual release with a guy.

Determined to suppress my gay cravings, instead of handing them over to God like I should have, I began making phone calls to erotic hotlines. I engaged in inappropriate conversations with men and got my pleasurable fix from them. I regarded my behavior as immoral and believed God probably gazed down on me in disappointment, but I couldn't get enough. Each time my mind conjured images, I called those hotlines and sought temporary pleasure from them.

Soon, my parents received an obscenely high phone bill and confronted me.

"You racked up a $400 bill calling hotlines, Nick?" My stepdad slammed the paper on the table in front of me. I gazed at the long log of 1-900 numbers and merely sighed. "Don't just sit there. You have some serious explaining to do. What in the world is going on with you, Nick?"

"Tell us why you're calling these disgusting numbers, Nicklaus!" Mom added.

"I'm sorry, all right?" I lowered my eyes and clutched my head. "God, I'm so sorry. I didn't mean for it to get out of hand. I didn't mean for that bill to get that high. I've been dealing with — ugh, I can't believe I'm saying this."

Mom placed a calm hand on my shoulder. "Dealing with what, Nicklaus?"

"Homosexual thoughts and feelings," I barely whispered. My stepdad gasped, and Mom released a whimper that sounded like a cracked note. "It's been going on since high school. It started with Jace, from church, but only a few times. Then I met this guy Marcos in college. I've been trying to live right, but I can't stop. It's like I'm imprisoned by sexual desires and stuff I know I shouldn't do. I know calling the hotlines was bad. I didn't know how to stop."

Nearly every secret I'd ever kept from my parents spilled from my tongue. It was a long time coming, and after that $400 bill, I felt like I owed them an explanation. They deserved to know the real reason behind my college departure and my need to start over elsewhere.

"Nicklaus, no." Mom dropped to the seat beside me, and J.J. hung his head. "No, no, no, no — this isn't supposed to happen to you. How could this happen? How could I not see?"

A mixture of shame and defensiveness filled my heart. "I can't help my feelings, Mom. I shouldn't have acted on them, and that's made it harder for me to reject them. They're strong."

"You know this is wrong, Nick." J.J. shook his head at me. "This is *sick*, son. This isn't who your mother raised you to be. This is completely against everything I've tried to influence you to be. This isn't right, Nick. This isn't right at all. God doesn't like this."

"We'll get through this," Mom breathed. "We won't tell *anyone*. Understand? We'll fix it. I don't know how, but you can always deal with this, Nicklaus. God can take this away."

I can't be fixed, I wanted to yell. *Why would God even*

consider taking this away after all I've done against him? HE WON'T! I'm messed up. This is just something I'm going to have to deal with for the rest of my life. Mom and J.J. don't get that. They'll never get it.

I bowed my head in disgrace, cringing at their words. I considered myself such a failure and embarrassment. There I sat, slumped over and scared, shattering their "good Christian boy" image of me. I understood why they didn't want my secret to get out. They were leaders in the church. Who knew how folks would judge them? I understood why they wanted to keep it "hush, hush." Their reaction still stung, though.

I wished Mom could have been more compassionate and J.J. more understanding, but they couldn't. They didn't know how it felt to be in my shoes, and *I got that.*

I never held that against them, though. My parents didn't stop loving me that day, either. They simply wanted me to be the man they always deemed I was. A man who could sincerely love and care for a woman someday. A man who could walk in the plan they believed God already had mapped out for his life. The sort of man they believed God created me to be.

Following that deep discussion with my parents, I forced myself to become more involved in church. I figured if I catapulted myself into church activities, then my mind wouldn't be so idle. And if my mind wasn't idle, it wouldn't randomly ponder inappropriate thoughts. My homosexual feelings weren't completely gone. I still harbored attraction toward males. I even began viewing pornography online, even though I tried hard to stay away from it.

I kept my secrets well hidden. I became leader of the church singing team, joined a Christian singles group to meet girls and acted like I had no problems at all. Again, I lived a lie while pretending to live totally for God.

Repeatedly, I asked God to send me a wife. I believed if I fell in love with a girl then my homosexual feelings would wholly go away. I just knew she could take away my desire to view gay pornography.

I pictured myself falling in love with a nice young lady in her early 20s — someone with a devout relationship with Christ and a forgiving heart. I knew my wife would need a forgiving heart to be with someone like me — a guy with what I regarded as a spotted past.

That's when Scarlett joined the singles group. Before I even met her, I'd heard she was a great singer, and I planned on persuading her to join the singing team at church. But when I laid eyes on her, the singing team just vanished from my mind. She stood in the middle of our church's Fall Festival talking to my sister Ingrid.

"Wow," I said to myself. "She's a really pretty girl."

Just then a shiver ran through me as I stared at her from across the room. I couldn't believe I found her attractive.

I'd never been able to regard women in a romantic manner, but with Scarlett, I could just picture going on dates with her and getting to know her. I could *see* her as my girlfriend. And that awed me. *God* awed me. *This has to be his doing,* I thought. *He's sending me the wife who will cure me from this sickness within me.*

Scarlett and I talked during the festival and quickly realized how much we had in common. Like me, she loved music. Like me, she was into theater and drama. Like me, she was chasing after God and striving to live like Jesus. I believed Scarlett was just too good to be true, so I started doubting my possible future with her.

Whoa! Man, I really like this girl, I thought. *There's no way she'll like me, though. If she knew of the things I've done, there's no way she'd ever want to deal with me. I might as well stick myself in the friend zone before I give her a chance to reject me.*

That's exactly what I did.

Soon, Scarlett and I became best friends. People often asked us why we wouldn't just date, because we seemed like the perfect match. I'd simply blush at their question and allow Scarlett to answer with a simple, "Oh, Nick? We're just cool. It's not like that with us."

She had no idea how badly I wanted it to be "like that" with us. My feelings for Scarlett were different than anything I'd ever come across. They were real emotions. I didn't merely lust after her and want to dive into some crazy physical relationship with her. I didn't think of her as just this object for me to release sexual desire. Pornography, my experiences with Jace and Marcos and the hotline stage I went through were nothing like my feelings for Scarlett.

Scarlett was a valued gift from God, and I truly

believed that. After I asked her out twice, and she declined twice, she finally gave me a chance. We dated, and on our first anniversary of dating, we got engaged. I thought about telling her about my past, but I couldn't bring myself to do it. I thought she'd immediately leave me when she found it.

This is the woman I love, I argued with myself. *I can't divulge my messy past to her. I can't tell her about my pornography problems.* No matter how many times I reminded myself I could never tell her, God must have had another plan, because one day I just blurted it out.

"You know, you can't expect me to always be happy." I looked at Scarlett in the driver's seat as I rested my head against the cold window. "That's not me. You think it is, but it's not."

"Huh?" Scarlett turned sharply. "What are you talking about?"

"I'm just saying," I stressed. "I act like this unfazed, cool and happy-go-lucky guy, but I'm not like that all the time. I deal with crap, too. Did you ever think of that? I have feelings that I don't want. I do things that I hate, but I can't seem to stop. I'm not always okay!"

"Whoa, Nick." Scarlett flicked a glance at me. "You need to calm down. You are obviously taking your anger out on me. I have no idea what you're going on about."

"Of course, you don't! I've never told you. I've never revealed the homosexual feelings and attraction toward men that I've bottled up for years. You don't know anything about that! Nobody really knows but my parents, and they don't get it. I've done things that would make you cringe, Scarlett. I have secrets that would make you walk away from me in a heartbeat."

"WHAT?" Scarlett braked at a stoplight and whipped her head toward me. "What homosexual feelings? What attraction? Where is all this coming from?"

"I … I just …"

She waited for me to answer, but my tongue suddenly locked. I couldn't believe I'd blurted out my secret. In that moment, I hated my big mouth for outing me. I didn't even know why or how I could suddenly drop a huge bombshell on her like that.

"Well, don't stop now, Nick!" Scarlett shouted. "What secrets are you talking about?"

I told her everything. I had no choice. From my childhood insecurities to my teenage struggles, my wild college days to my secret pornography addiction. I let it all out.

She eyed me cautiously. "Are you still dealing with this, Nick? Did you overcome it or what? I mean, you've given your life to Christ, right? God has set you free from that, right?"

I lied.

"Yes!" I nodded. "God has definitely freed me from the captivity I was in. I used to be that way, but I'm over that. I made some horrible decisions, I know that now. I gave in to those feelings instead of giving them over to God in the first place. I always knew I was never meant to live that gay lifestyle. Sometimes, I just get agitated. Probably because I don't have anyone to really talk to about it. I just get overwhelmed and frustrated, you know?"

"But you're sure homosexuality and pornography aren't a problem for you anymore?"

"Yes, Scarlett. I promise you. I'm over it. I just didn't feel right marrying you without telling you about my past. God took all that nonsense away. You don't have to worry."

Months later, Scarlett and I married. I thought I'd automatically be cured from my unwanted desires, but two months into the marriage, they crept back into my life. I started having cravings to watch gay pornography. I found myself looking at men longer than I should have. After I'd been sneaking around and watching online videos, Scarlett caught me and justifiably flipped out.

"What is this, Nick?" She banged her purse on the desk beside me and swiveled the monitor to face her. Her mouth dropped in disgust before clicking out of the browser. "Are you kidding me? You're looking at men sleeping together? I thought this was taken care of. You said God took these sort of desires away. What is wrong with you?"

Silence.

"ANSWER ME, NICK! ANSWER ME, NOW!"

I swallowed. "I can't. I don't have anything to say." I bowed my head toward the keyboard and shook it. "I'm so sorry, Scarlett. Those feelings I told you about, they haven't gone away completely. I lied to you. God, I'm so sorry, baby."

"No." Scarlett clutched at her hair and groaned. "No, no, no, that's not good enough. Sorry isn't good enough, Nick! Why'd you let me marry you if you were still having these gay feelings? How could you do this to me?"

"I know." I hopped from my computer chair and faced Scarlett. "I thought our marriage would cure me because I really do love you and you only. I need you to know that. I just can't shake this. And I know it looks horrible, and you probably don't believe a word I'm saying, but I don't want this in my life. I need help, Scarlett."

Scarlett and I ran to our parents for help with my issue. Her parents never judged or scolded me, they just loved me and advised that I seek counseling from our pastor. My parents agreed with them, wanting me to trust God with my problems. I repeatedly told them I wasn't a homosexual man, I was just struggling with homosexual feelings. I loved Scarlett. I didn't want anyone but her.

Even with their encouraging words, I didn't believe I'd ever get rid of my problem. I wanted complete freedom from my habits, but I believed I didn't deserve for God to give me that. Just like I'd broken Scarlett's heart, I believed I'd hurt God even more. I believed he despised my double life and that it severely disappointed him when I turned to sexual immorality instead of giving my dilemma to him. I believed it irked him that I walked around like this cool Christian guy who had it all together, and yet I relished viewing filthy films when no one was around.

Scarlett and I separated for a few months. I lived in hotels, while she stayed at our home. We still attended church and continued with our regular Sunday duties, but we weren't attached at the hip like we'd always been. Folks noticed the distance between us, but we didn't divulge the nature of our problems. With people witnessing our marriage crumble, I knew I needed to really trust God with my struggles and allow him to change my mind. I asked him to create a clean heart within me.

Like a stubborn mule, I still didn't fully relinquish the matter to God. I continuously thought of ways to fix it myself. I ensured I was never alone, so I didn't have an urge to browse the Internet. I kept telling myself that Scarlett and I should have children sooner than later. *With kids running around, I won't have time to think about watching pornography,* I rationalized.

Though I thought of tactics to keep me from slipping up, those tactics sometimes failed. And when Scarlett and I got back together, a week before our third anniversary, I goofed up. She caught me in the middle of having explicit conversations with men online, and we had a huge fight. For a while, I stayed with a friend of mine or slept on my parents' couch. Ingrid and Logan didn't think much of my sudden presence, they just thought I was in the dog house with Scarlett for something minor. They didn't know what was actually happening between us.

Months later, Scarlett and I finally reconciled, and we decided to seek the counseling from our pastors that our parents initially advised. Our pastor tried to talk to me about triggers that caused me to delve into my habit.

He discussed the importance of not watching certain

television shows or anything else that might implant images in my mind that could make me want to surf the Net for porn. He gave us activities to do together that he said would steer me away from that lifestyle.

The only problem I had with his counseling was that he never talked about handing my problem over to God and allowing God to step in and cure me. He never gave me any scriptures to strengthen me against my lustful thoughts. I felt like we weren't getting to the crux of the matter.

And I know we didn't. Because when I slipped up and watched pornography, Scarlett caught me a third time. We met with our parents again, hoping they could offer a solution.

"I am completely over this, Nick." Scarlett shook her head and shrugged her shoulders. She'd given up on me, and I knew it. "You've broken my heart too many times. I'm done. There is no coming back from this. Our next step is divorce. I can't trust you."

"You have to make a choice, Nicklaus." Mom regarded me from across the table. "You need to decide what you want. If you choose to continue with this behavior, you will lose your entire family. As your Christian mother and Christian stepfather, we cannot stand behind you if you choose to live this way. Scarlett cannot be your wife."

My mother was right. Just like in college, I believe God spoke through my mother and captured my attention. It was like he was telling me, *Time is up, Nick. Make a choice.*

OUT OF THESE ASHES

I knew that living as an openly gay man in our society wouldn't be all rainbows, parades and dance parties. People judge. They could dismiss me with their looks and words. Family and friends would be unable to support me and would be displeased with that way of living. The biggest hurt of all would be believing God was displeased, though. When I weighed all that, I knew it was time to give it up. So, I started seeing a Christian counselor, Dr. Winchester.

Talking to Dr. Winchester proved to be so stress-free, helpful and promising. His honesty and aspiration to help eliminate my unwanted feelings didn't go unnoticed. I recognized the sincerity in Dr. Winchester. He told me my journey wouldn't be easy, but if I was dedicated, we'd make it there. I believed God put him in my life for a reason. So did Scarlett. I talked to him freely, and he listened to every word I said.

"I hate the fact that I can see an advertisement for something, and my mind instantly creates an inappropriate thought from it." I wrung my hands as I sat opposite him. "I hate the fact that I can't go to a beach without feeling an attraction toward shirtless guys. Sometimes I try to concentrate on the women in bikinis. I feel like that's better than looking at the guys."

Dr. Winchester tilted his head in thought. "I believe you know that isn't right, Nicklaus. Deep down, you know that isn't a good tactic. That's precisely why we're going to discuss some tactics that will help you. But it's going to be a constant battle, Nicklaus. This can't go away overnight.

It didn't develop overnight, so it will take time to get over it."

"I never feel good after viewing pornography. I feel so dumb for giving in. It's like I have no control over my actions."

"That will change, Nicklaus. Remember that purity precedes power. The more you abstain from these feelings and desires, the more powerful you will become to completely overcome this. That power comes from the Lord. That's why it's important you stay close to him."

As a Christian counselor, Dr. Winchester made certain that I understood there was an enemy who wished to kill, steal and destroy everything God has ever created. That included me. The devil didn't want me to walk in the purpose God laid out for me. I believed that the devil planted homosexuality in my life to hinder me from being the man God wanted me to be.

Overall, it took nine months to rebuild my relationship with God, repair my marriage with Scarlett and completely let go of all homosexual desires within me. It was the hardest I ever had to work. I used accountability software to block dubious Web sites. My parents, Scarlett and her parents received email notifications if there was any questionable activity happening on my computer. I not only had to answer to God, I had to answer to other people, too.

Dr. Winchester taught me that I needed to "put on the whole armor of God" to fight my unwanted feelings. That meant concentrating on Jesus — reading the Bible daily, memorizing scripture and speaking it from my heart, praying to God and staying in constant communication with him. I knew I wouldn't always be able to drop to my knees and talk to God whenever I struggled, but I could consume my thoughts with God. And I was determined to do just that.

❧❧❧

Seven years later, my marriage with Scarlett was stronger than ever before.

I became free of the desire to secretly view pornography, something that once ruled my behavior. I became free of the secrets and lies. I became free of the homosexual thoughts and attraction toward men.

I became free of it all.

Scarlett and I continued to cultivate our marriage with Jesus at the center of our lives. My wife came to trust me not to break her heart again. We had children, and they had a father they could depend on to keep their family intact.

Although I experienced such a rough time before joining Real Life Church, my church has given me a voice to declare my story to so many people. I can tell so many that God has changed me. With him, I overcame who I was and allowed God to transform me into the man I believe he always wanted me to be. And I became the man I wanted to be.

THE GREAT LOVE
The Story of Sofie
Written by Laura Paulus

"Hurry up! You are so slow and stupid."

I tried to move quickly.

Nothing ever seemed to be enough. I constantly let her down. I could not remember a time in my 9 years that I'd ever pleased my mother.

"I told you to get ready!" she screamed at me. "Why are you not moving?"

Suddenly, I felt myself pushed to the floor. I fell on my stomach and felt heavy pressure on my back as she sat on me. I lay pinned there as she screamed and pummeled me. I felt the pounding of her fists and heard the dull thuds they made as they connected with my back.

Mortified, I realized that my friend who had spent the night could see it all. *I finally got the nerve up to have a friend over only to have my secret revealed.* Now she knew about our family issues.

Eventually, Mom's fury abated, and she got off of me. She left the room. Scared to even look at my friend, I turned and met her glance.

"Look, she is sick. She can't help it. We need to keep this between us. Please do not tell anyone at school about this."

While this was my everyday life, I felt horror that my

friend knew I had so much wrong with me. She probably thought I was worthless. Clearly, I was unloved. I would need to be more careful and not let her or any other friend see the way my mom treated me again. *I am sure that only my mother acts like this.* The other moms I had observed did not do such mean things.

ぺぺぺ

My parents met at a park where they both worked cleaning up trash. Barely together at the time of my conception, they could not abort since they realized too late that Mom was pregnant.

My mom hardly seemed the prime candidate for motherhood. She suffered from schizophrenia and took several medications that were not recommended during pregnancy. My mother smoked heavily as well. She'd had my brother Sam eight years before, but she had several abortions before me and smoked heavily.

My parents decided to give their romance a shot and moved in together. They fought even from the beginning of their relationship — even arguing at their wedding a few years later when I turned 3.

Once, my paternal grandmother told me that my mom could be quite aggressive with me as a baby. Grandma said that my mom would yell at me and get very upset if I cried too much.

Evidently, when I was 6 months old, I had a broken bone in my upper thigh. My mother told people that I had crawled out of the crib and broken it, but the doctor who treated me did not think the break appeared consistent with her story. He notified the county social workers, who made a visit to our home, but they were unable to determine the reason for the break. I've always wondered if my mom dropped me or broke my leg when she was frustrated with me.

Due to the instability of my parents and their marriage, my family moved out to the country to live with my dad's parents. I spent most of my time with my grandfather. He would ask me to go out with him every evening to pull his truck into the garage. But then he would start doing things he shouldn't have — not with me or any child. He started getting me alone at other times, too.

This went on for several years. My dad's sister became suspicious and began to watch more closely. Soon I started school where we discussed good touch and bad touch. I told the teacher what my grandfather had been doing. My parents were notified, and my aunt shared her observations.

Charges were filed, and my grandfather went to court. I had to tell the court about my grandfather's actions. I had to describe the details while he sat in front of me. It was an awful experience. My dad begged me not to send my grandfather to jail. I knew that telling the truth made me a bad person to my family. Somehow, the charges were dropped.

No one made any moves to protect me or change

things, except that we did move out of my grandparents' house. We continued to go to their home and visit them, though. At every visit, when it came time to go, my father insisted I say goodbye to my grandfather.

"Sofie, give your grandfather a hug and kiss before we go."

Not the type of child to make trouble, I would try to avoid the situation and slip out the door and not have to embrace the man who had done such awful things to me.

"Sofie! Show your grandfather respect, and give him a kiss."

Trapped, I obeyed and cringed the whole time. I felt abandoned and unsafe. Even at a young age, I felt that no one fought for me. These terrible acts had occurred, but life just continued on as if they never had.

I also got noticed by my cousin on my mom's side. This cousin frequently spent the night with our family since he and Sam were the same age. Like my grandfather, he found opportunities to get me alone and do things I didn't want him to do.

I never told anyone because he said things that felt threatening to me. I feared the consequences of reporting. He and my brother were close.

No one seemed to catch on because most of his attention happened at night when everyone slept. Sometimes it happened during the day, too, but my parents never paid attention or caught on. I didn't fight since my cousin would threaten to tell my family mean things about me if I did.

This went on for years. I later found out that he had also targeted another cousin a little bit younger than me.

Three more family members sexually abused me throughout my childhood but none to the extent that my grandfather and cousin had. Even though I did not fully understand all that had gone on, I knew enough to know that these things were not normal. I wondered if it meant that something was wrong with me. I had low self-esteem and felt shameful and dirty from a young age. They tested me for possible placement in special education as I struggled in school, but I did not end up qualifying. I felt worthless.

My parents continued to fight. Most of their fights revolved around the topic of money. They would get so heated in their arguments that they often threw items at each other. And if not fighting, they were off partying. Regular activities in our home included my dad doing cocaine and my mom drinking.

Thankfully, I had my brother Sam. Not only did we get along well, but he took care of me. Sam woke me up in the morning, helped me to find clothes to wear, made sure that I ate and helped me get to school on time.

I got picked on a lot in school because my mom did not take care of me or brush my hair. My brother did his best, but I still looked like a mess when I went to school. The kids made fun of me, and they called me weird. I could not argue with them, because I felt weird. I felt like I had a defect. I only wanted people to like me.

Sam took care of me after school, too. He often took

me along with him and his friends when they hung out. My mom could be unpredictable and mean to me. Sam did not want anything bad to happen to me.

After I turned 8, the fighting became too much, and my parents decided to divorce. My mom had some severe schizophrenic episodes, so I stayed with my dad while Mom moved out. My brother left and went to live with a friend.

Immediately after my mom moved out, my dad invited his girlfriend and her kids to live with us. I ended up sleeping on the couch, while her kids got my room. I felt like a guest in my own home. I also felt lonely since my ally Sam had left.

Like many divorced parents, mine used their kid to get at each other. My mom would make me call my dad and say that I could not come back. Both would say negative things about the other and try to get me to take their side.

I moved back in with my mom when I turned 9. Living with my mom involved chaos and turmoil. Due to the schizophrenia, my mom had some odd behaviors. Unpredictably, she would laugh for hours. She had no reason to laugh, but it would continue on for long periods of time. I knew to stay out of the way as much as I could.

One time Sam came home for a visit. He brought his girlfriend with him, and they shared the news that they were having a baby. Mom freaked out. She began to hear voices on the TV saying things to her. No one else in the room could hear anything. I continued trying to watch my cartoons.

"Sofie, turn that off. They are saying such terrible things, and I can't listen to it anymore."

I jumped up to turn the TV off, hoping that would be enough to calm my mom down. Instead, her voice continued to rise hysterically as she began pacing.

"Sam, you have to get that thing out of here! Take it outside."

She meant the TV.

"Mom, calm down. We are upstairs, and that thing is huge. It is crazy for me to take it out! Just calm down, and let Sofie finish her cartoons."

"Don't tell me to calm down. You think you are so smart, and I am crazy, but I'm not. I know what they are saying on there. Get it out of here now!"

My brother knew it did not help anything reasoning with her, so he lugged the beast of a TV down the stairs and put it outside. Sam had been able to protect me from understanding the extent of Mom's mental illness, but watching my brother carry the TV down the stairs helped me realize just how bad it was.

I had memories of Mom's parents holding her down as she freaked out at various times, but Sam always seemed to make it all better. He would tell me, "Mommy doesn't feel well and needs to go away for a while." And they'd send her to the psychiatric hospital for a while.

But since Sam wasn't around as much, I'd experienced more and more of my mom's unpredictability. She would often leave me by myself for several days at a time and sometimes as long as a week. I wandered around looking for my mom all over town. Since Mom used our money for alcohol, I would be left alone with nothing to eat but saltine crackers and occasionally applesauce. I did not know any phone numbers, so I could not call anyone for help.

I would get myself to school, but often I looked messy since I did not have clean clothes. Yet, no one ever fully knew all that went on in my family. Social workers continued to come in and out of the home over the years, but nothing ever really changed.

Even after my friend came over and saw my mom sit on top of me, hitting me, nothing changed. My friend did not tell, or at least no one did anything about it. I just stopped having friends over after that. It worked out fine since I really did not have very many friends, and none of my friends were popular. I got picked on enough already. I could not chance anyone else seeing how crazy my life truly could be.

As time went on, my mom's drinking and episodes got worse. She would yell at me, hit and kick me. When Sam came around, my mom did not abuse me physically, but she had no problem verbally insulting me all of the time.

One time, she pulled a knife on my brother. Attempting to protect himself, he restrained her until the cops arrived after neighbors called them. My brother ended up getting arrested since my mom accused him of attacking her. I begged to be able to go stay with Sam's girlfriend that night. I felt too scared to be with my mom.

The Great Love

❧❧❧

I moved back in with Dad, hoping he would offer more stability. My dad worked in his garage on cars during his time off, while I did my best to cook, clean and care for the home. My dad expected this from me. He also expected that I stop failing and do well in school, but only after I made sure that everything in the house got done.

Shortly after moving in with Dad, my brother began struggling. He started drinking too much. He got into a fight with his girlfriend and pushed her, so she left him. It seemed he did not know what to do with his emotions. I could see him reverting to the behavior that had been modeled for him his whole life. He began hurting himself and those closest to him.

Sam had always wanted to make people happy and would do all he could to get a laugh, but he became someone who went to work and then came home and drank. He would sit down in a chair in the living room and stare at the TV. He would not look up and greet me when I came in the room. He just withdrew into himself.

He seemed overwhelmed and was obviously struggling financially. He had numerous tickets from drinking and driving and soon lost his license. I wanted to help him like he had always helped me. But I had no idea where to start.

❧❧❧

I was 13 when Sam had to attend AA and a few other court-mandated meetings in the nearby town of Lansing.

It took at least a half an hour to drive there, and he did not have a car. Sam would often ride his bike back and forth to Lansing or just stay for the week with friends there.

One day, Sam decided to drive, even though he had a suspended license. A witness later described noticing my brother driving extremely slowly on the freeway. Sam suddenly fell over, as if picking up something or passing out, and the car veered toward the guardrail. It seemed like he tried to hit the brake but hit the accelerator instead. The car sped up and hit the barrier. His head hit the dashboard. Just like that, he was brain dead.

The evening of the accident, I heard a tapping on my window. At first I thought it might be Sam since I had not seen him for almost a week, and I had just been thinking about him. He often tapped on my window when he got home so I could let him in. When I looked out, I noticed my aunt, and it surprised me. I ran to let her in the front door. I could tell by the look on her face that something had happened.

"What's wrong?"

"Sam has been in an accident, and we need to get to the hospital."

It is a car accident, but that doesn't mean it is really bad.

I went and told my dad, and we left. He remained completely silent on the way there, while I prayed frantically in my head. I asked for a sign that my brother would live. In my heart, I felt a voice say, *No, he is not going to make it.* I shoved that voice away.

As we walked into the hospital waiting room, we saw all of Sam's friends and a lot of our relatives there crying. Feeling numb, I told myself that Sam would only be staying in the hospital for the night.

Time stood still, and then everything moved in slow motion. My dad and an old girlfriend of Sam's, who I remained close to, went in with me to see Sam. I held his hand and looked at him. I could hear the sounds of the life-support machines working to keep him alive. His head, bandaged and swollen, looked alarming, but the rest of him looked fine.

"Hold on, you're gonna make it. I know you are."

I just couldn't say goodbye to him. That would make it all real. My heart felt devastated. My brother had walked through life with me and knew how it all felt. No one else got it all like he did, and I needed him.

I longed for Sam to recover, but it did not happen. My family made the decision to take him off of life support the next day. Everyone was in shock. Even my mom, who typically got hysterical, had little to no emotion. She calmly made decisions and did what needed to be done.

≈≈≈

The calm did not last. Mom began drinking heavily and having more frequent schizophrenic episodes after losing my brother. She started going downhill quickly, and I knew the responsibility to care for her fell to me. I left my dad's place and went to take care of her.

My dad accused me of abandoning him and making him feel like a bad dad. He told me if I left then I could not come back. I felt like I had to go because Mom needed me. All the stability in my life seemed to vanish after Dad disowned me. First Sam, then Dad.

Instead of moving in with Mom directly, I decided to move in with a cousin who had always been like a sister to me. I knew that I could live with her and still be close enough to my mom to help out.

I continued to try to make things right with Dad. I would call him, and he would hang up. After a few years, he lost his house and got into meth. Sometimes he would call me.

"Dad, I am so sorry. I love you."

"I don't think you do."

This conversation happened many times.

I started drinking and smoking marijuana. I went to a party at age 14 where I had too much to drink and ended up sleeping with a man in his 20s. I did not fully realize what had happened until the next day. I felt so dirty and ashamed.

I decided that I wanted to take control of what happened to my body. I started dressing in shorter shirts and taking more care in my appearance. I felt confident. I knew that I looked older and could get guys to notice me. I enjoyed getting attention. I learned to play the drums and sang in coffee shops and bars. While it felt good at times, I still felt defective inside and of little value.

I dated a few guys who were into drugs. I wanted to fix

them. I was ultimately searching to be a better person myself, but it was easier to attempt to improve the guys I dated. These relationships did not work out.

かかか

My freshman year of high school felt like a fresh start. I moved to a new school and embraced the chance to reinvent myself. I decided that I would not be the weird girl I had always been. I began stealing clothes from stores so that I could dress more fashionably. I bleached my hair blond.

I noticed Josh right away. A friend pointed him out to me on the first day and told me that a lot of girls liked him. When I saw him, I had this feeling that we belonged together. Josh sold weed, and everyone seemed to like him. After a while, we started dating.

After we had been dating a while, another incident happened with the cousin who had abused me over the years. One night, he attempted to sexually abuse me and another cousin we were staying with while we slept. My other cousin told on him, and just like before, things got swept under the carpet. We were told to never speak of it again. I felt like justice didn't exist for me.

Once again, feelings of worthlessness flooded me. Josh could tell something seemed wrong and asked me about it. I told about all of the abuse. He stuck with me, and that surprised me. I expected him to leave, but instead, for the first time, someone other than my brother actually cared about me. It helped that Josh did not make me feel dirty about what had happened to me.

෧෧෧

In spite of all that had happened to me in my life, I often felt a connection with God. Even at a young age, I felt drawn to him. My maternal grandmother, Granny, told me about Jesus when I was young. Sam taught me about Jesus as well. In fact, I learned the most from him. I knew that the person I had become was not who I needed to be. I wanted something more in my life.

As my relationship with Josh continued to be steady, I decided to go to church. I started attending one nearby and got really involved with the youth group. I invited Josh, who continued to sell weed and to be involved in a bad crowd. I told him that I could feel something inside of me changing, and I wanted him to experience it, as well. He declined several times and then finally showed up high. I didn't care, because I just wanted him to come.

Josh had a life-changing experience when he met a guy at the church who appeared to be really poor. This man did not fall under the cool guy category or have money. But he seemed content and had something that Josh did not have. And Josh had it all: the cool image, lots of money from selling drugs, all the girls liked him, etc. But he felt incomplete. Josh asked the guy what he had and how to get it, and the guy encouraged him to keep coming and find out. Josh came sober the next time. Josh saw the contradiction between what society prescribes and what God provides. He decided that this guy was onto something.

Over time, we both learned more about God's love. We decided that the time had come to have personal relationships with God, so we prayed and told God we believed in him and accepted the love that he freely offered us. We both completely changed. Others began to recognize the change, as well, and not only classmates but teachers and administrators at school.

Josh began to wear homemade T-shirts with scripture verses on them. He carried his Bible around. He shared about his faith with his friends. I decided to start doing better in school, so he started encouraging me to study, and we studied together. My grades slowly improved.

❧❧❧

I unexplainably began putting on weight. I gained close to 50 pounds in one year. I had been changing on the inside, but I still placed high value on my looks. The weight gain shook me. I feared that Josh would walk out on me, but he did not.

We had started attending church activities on Wednesday nights. Soon we attended on Sundays at a different church that we loved. We felt we could be real there and not have to worry about maintaining any type of image. We could go to learn and not have all of the answers.

During winter break our sophomore year, a couple of the teachers from the church prayed over me for the upcoming semester. As a result, something changed in me. I decided that I no longer wanted to be a failure. I wanted to succeed and make something of my life. I did not want my family to be right. They had been saying all along that I would be pregnant by age 16 and would drop out of school. I applied myself and never failed another class.

I had felt empty inside for so long. But as I pursued God, the hole in my heart seemed to fill up. In the love of Christ, I finally found the completeness I sought. I felt peace and realized that his love was exactly why I existed and what I had been made for. It made everything that I had gone through worth it. Those things kept pushing me forward to find meaning in my life and led me to Jesus. I only wish that I could have told Sam about God's love.

അൎൎൎ

I graduated from high school. Thanks to extra classes and summer school, I had been able to raise my GPA. The school surprised me with an award for my improvement. I felt validated. People saw me. My dad had re-entered my life, and he made it to my graduation. I could tell he felt pride for my accomplishments. Josh's family also cheered me on at graduation. I enjoyed having those important people there for such an important day.

During senior year, Josh and I raised money to be able to go to a soup kitchen in Mexico to serve for a week.

Much of the money came from fellow students who donated into a can that I carried around. We ended up raising so much money that we were able to pay for our trip, as well as donate extra to the missionaries at the soup kitchen. This trip served as a time for me to experience something outside of myself, my environment and my family.

That fall, Josh and I participated in a program that emphasized ministry. Participants could not date anyone for one year in order to focus on their relationship with the Lord. As Josh and I took the year off from dating, we developed our friendship and got to know each other in a new way.

This time allowed us to work through all of the changes that we had come through during our time of dating. Along with the changes, some issues came to the surface.

We worked hard to maintain a healthy relationship, and he remained my best friend.

During our time participating in the ministry program, friends started the church we still attend. Years later, Real Life Church is growing and doing well. We love being a part of a God-loving, caring, beautiful, imperfect community.

❧❧❧

After we helped our friends start the church, Josh and I began attending a local Christian college where I pursued the study of psychology. I did well in this and finally enjoyed school.

Josh and I had tried to break up many times over our dating years, but we always ended up back together. Even when we were frustrated and wanted to stop dating, we just couldn't. It seemed like God meant for us to be together.

We married several months after I turned 21, and it is still one of the best decisions that I ever made.

Josh is an amazing husband who makes me feel worthy of love. We both feel like completely different people in our marriage than when we first started dating.

Two years into our marriage, we had our first amazing son. I finished up all but two semesters of my bachelor's degree shortly after having him. I was thrilled, never having thought that I would get to attend college.

My mom started coming around more after our son's birth. She remained the same but would visit and help me out. My dad called and visited as much as his job allowed him between assignments out of town.

A few years later, I became pregnant with our daughter. I had prayed for my little girl and felt fortunate that God blessed me with our kids. God helped me to break the patterns of abuse in my family. My own children would not have to grow up in the conditions that I had.

About this time, my mom began to change drastically. Her behavior went beyond her normal unpredictability. We worried that she had started doing drugs. She withdrew from our lives, but we continued to pray for her.

At 26, I had our youngest child. As a mother, I felt inadequate at times because I never had good parenting modeled for me, but God continued to give me strength and grace. Amazed at how far God brought me, I couldn't believe all that I had been given. I believe every step was possible because of God's love. I didn't deserve it, but God gave me the chance to have a healthy family.

I love the verse in the Bible that reads, "And do not be conformed to this world, but be transformed by the renewing of your mind, that you may prove what is the good and acceptable and perfect will of God" (Romans 12:2 NKJV). I fully believed that God had the ability to change the way we think in order to bring healing. One day I suddenly realized that had happened for me. God had completely shifted my thought processes. I began to be more positive and more readily offered love to others, just as Jesus had offered love to me.

I learned how to be a loving wife and mother. Real Life Church provided a strong foundation for me to lean on. I had others to depend on who made me stronger. We leaned on each other and on God. We knew that we were not necessarily qualified to do the things God called us to do together, but that left so much more room for him to work through us.

God showed me how to be a better mom. He gave me strength in my weakness. Even though my childhood was not perfect, he created something beautiful from the ashes.

Dad continued to be involved in our lives, and our relationship healed. I knew that he loved me, and I prayed that he would find hope and healing in a relationship with God.

I remembered the beatings I took from Mom as a child and still didn't hold her mental illness or alcoholism against her. Her sickness prevented her from having a healthy relationship with me. She continued to struggle, but I loved her still.

తతత

"He is jealous for me, loves like a hurricane, and I am a tree bending beneath the weight of his wind and mercy."

Tears streamed down my face as Josh, the kids and I stood up singing in our worship service. The music swelled as the truth flooded my mind: *I am bent and molded by his love and mercy. God loved me despite everything. Even when I felt worthless, dirty, undeserving. God understands me. He can fill every void.*

As I sang out, I thought about how God can speak life into things that seem too far gone — dead. If he brought Jesus back from the dead, surely he can fill us with life.

I know I'll never fully understand God's love because it is so great, but I get it more than I used to. God sought me out and wanted to love me. His love is pure. And he gives it to me, even though I have seen and experienced awful things. I have found his great love, and it is so amazing.

THE VERDICT
The Story of Larkin
Written by Audrey Jackson

My pressed button-down cotton shirt soaked up my perspiration as I sat staring ahead at the judge. I reached up and loosened my necktie, pulling the knot back and forth until it came undone.

From the wooden bench where I sat, I locked eyes on one of the jury members, sitting to the right of the witness stand. To the left, the judge in his judicial attire sat staring over at a series of images being shown on a screen. My eyes shifted to the screen, displaying graphic images of my father's bullet wounds.

I could feel my sister touch my hand. She lowered her gaze, away from the photographs. I looked from the screen's detailed images to the left side of the courtroom. I could only see his profile — sitting there staring ahead. And as I stared, it hit me.

I'm sitting 10 feet away from the man who killed my father.

෧෧෧

As kids, we were taught to appreciate everything we had. I guess that's because we didn't have a whole lot. Sometimes I wondered why we didn't have certain things that other kids in school had. New clothes. Toys. But it wasn't easy for my parents back then — making ends meet on one income.

I was the youngest of three. I had an older brother and sister, and we spent most of our childhood going back and forth between Mom's house and Dad's. They had gotten divorced, but they were amiable enough with one another. If they told us once, they told us a hundred times, "Learn from our mistakes." It was just one of those marriages that hadn't been right, and they couldn't work it out. Or at least that's how it seemed to me. And though our family struggled to make ends meet sometimes, I don't think any of us ever felt like either of our parents failed in giving us what we needed.

Mom gave us tradition and religion. She taught us to pray and respect our elders. I guess you would call her the "churchgoing" type. The sort of woman who was in the Baptist church building every time the doors were open. It was Mom who took us to Sunday school each week, and it was Mom who helped me whisper a prayer to Jesus when I was 8 years old.

I remember that moment so clearly. It was dark when she crept into our room, her footsteps soft and silent — like fog settling quietly in the early dawn.

"Mom," I whispered. "Come here."

She nestled in with us on top of the covers. "What is it, boys? It's time for bed."

"We think we want to ask Jesus into our hearts."

Even in the dimly lit room, I could see the corners of

her mouth turn up in a smile. "Do you boys think you understand what that means? To ask Jesus into your heart?"

"Yeah. I mean, it's just asking him to forgive the bad things we do and the hate and anger in our hearts. And believing that he died for us. And that he's God's son. And believing that he's always there."

"And do you believe all of those things?"

I paused, silently pondering as my brother lay beside me. "Yeah, Mom. I really do."

"Then let's pray together."

かみかみかみ

If Mom taught us about who God was and how to be respectful members of society, Dad was the one who taught us how to survive and glean from the wild all around us. Dad was a big man — about 6 feet, 3 inches tall and 230 pounds. And he loved to be outdoors. He taught us to pay attention to the pace of nature. To fish and hunt and not be afraid to do so. He taught us to provide for ourselves with what surrounded us. And though I didn't realize it at the time, being around Dad in those moments — those days out under the great big sky — became a milestone in my journey to becoming a man.

かみかみかみ

Dad's eyes were blue with a rim of gray around them. It was a fall day, and the colors of the trees reflected upon the water all around us. My brother Justin and I huddled in the bottom of the boat, looking over the edge. Dad crouched at the other end, showing my sister Leslie how to bait her hook. The aluminum-bottom boat floated slowly, almost motionlessly. It was as if time had stopped and we were the only people alive — living out the most relaxing, quiet day on the water.

"Ewww, Dad, I am not touching that worm," said Leslie, scrunching up her nose.

"Aw, come on now, Les — it's part of it. You can't be a great fisherman without learning to bait your hook." He reached around her and helped her slide the hook through the worm's side.

"Yuck, that's disgusting."

"Leslie — you're such a baby. Dad, let me try." I walked over slowly, bending my legs and steadying myself so as not to make the boat move any more than it had to.

"You think you can do it, Lark?"

"Oh, I've got it under control." Dad's hearty laugh bellowed out and echoed upon the pond. He tousled my hair with his large hand and drew me to his chest.

"All right, pal, go ahead and bait your hook and throw it out there. We've got to catch some fish for dinner or we aren't going to have anything to eat."

"Don't worry. We'll catch some here soon. I remember how you taught me to cast it out."

"Perfect, pal. You go at it then. I'm looking forward to my kiddos bringing home the bacon tonight."

The Verdict

❧❧❧

I was in high school when Dad packed up and moved to Montana. I think the land had always been calling his name. And though my siblings and I definitely felt the absence of Dad, we got through it somehow. We clung to the fact that Dad hadn't left because of a lack of love for us and to our faith in God, our heavenly father, who we believed loved us eternally.

Dad sent Christmas and birthday cards, but we didn't really talk to him much. I knew Dad loved the Lord and us, but sometimes it felt like he drifted a bit.

I considered myself a normal, decent teenager. I was involved in sports, athletic and a natural leader. I liked to be everyone's friend. And I liked to think that I had inherited a lot of that from Dad.

He was a strapping man, my father. An Army veteran who had served his country proudly. That was something I'd always hold on to whenever I missed him. I had some of him in me, so he was always there somehow.

Around the time I entered high school, I began to recognize the void Dad's absence created in my life. I wanted a man around — I wanted him. So I started calling him once a week or so. And though his influence was small, it made a big impact. Dad was struggling, and I felt like I was being an encouragement to him somehow — encouraging him to be the man I knew he had been to me as a kid.

"Hey, Dad, how's it going?" I said one day, holding the telephone up to my cheek.

"Oh, not too bad, kiddo. My neighbor's on my tail again about the lawn out back. The jerk just won't get off my back. I swear he complains about it three times a week. An idiot is what he is."

"Dad, you should just kill him with kindness. Then he won't have anything to get mad about, right? I don't know. He just sounds like a creep, to be honest. At least from everything you've said in the past."

"Yeah, yeah, I know, pal. You're right. So what's new with you?"

"Eh, not too much. Just school and practice. And I feel like God has been teaching me a lot lately."

There was a pause on the other end of the phone. "Oh, yeah?"

"Yeah, I mean, he's just always there, ya know? And it kind of just blows my mind. I mean, I've always believed in God. Since I was little. But up until recently I don't think I really ever understood how he's always there. Like, when I'm lonely or hurt or angry. He's always there."

"Yeah, it's pretty crazy to think about." He paused. "You're a great kid, Larkin. Becoming a great man. You keep being who you are and seeking after what you believe in. I want you to know that I love you."

"I love you, too, Dad."

"All right, well, tell your mom and brother and sister I said hi, if you see them. I'll talk to you soon."

"Yeah, okay. I'll talk to you later."

And both lines went silent as we hung up our phones.

The Verdict

࿐࿐࿐

I sat in Mom's house in the Upper Peninsula, next to Leslie. Mom sat in the blue La-Z-Boy chair next to my brother when the phone rang. I was on break from college, and we had all been sitting around chatting in the living room. Our shoes had come off early on, and we all sat around relaxing. It was nice to just be together.

"What do you guys want to do for dinner tonight?" Mom asked, walking across the room to pick up the ringing telephone.

"I'd be up for hamburgers," Leslie piped in.

"What about pizza?" I asked. Looking over across the room, I saw Mom's face turning white.

I knew something was wrong. My stomach felt like it dropped suddenly, the way a water balloon falls quickly and splats on the pavement when it's dropped from a balcony. *I wonder if it's Grandma. Maybe something's happened to her.* I looked over at my brother and sister, all of our eyes growing bigger as Mom slowly walked back over to our side of the room. She looked as if all of her limbs had gone numb.

"Mom," I said in a low voice. "What's going on?"

Large tears filled her eyes and started to pour over onto her cheeks.

"Your dad. He … he was shot by his neighbor. And he died." She doubled over, burying her head between her knees. Her back shook as she sobbed.

The moments after remain a blur. There are some

parts that I can't remember. What we said to one another. How long I wept into my hands. But then there are things I won't ever be able to forget. Things like the sound of my family's cries and wails, piercing my ears and heart. The feeling of panic in my gut. The deep chasm that suddenly formed inside of me. I can't explain to you what it feels like to lose a parent to murder. But for me it was almost like someone had taken my heart and wrung out every last drop of joy. I looked up at the ceiling, embracing Mom against my chest, and couldn't imagine what any of us would do moving forward.

How can we keep going when this has happened? And why would God allow him to die?

❧❧❧

The smell of the coffee made me sick. I sat there, my eyes stinging. I reached up my hand and rubbed my eyes, furrowing my brow as I shut them. A feeling of guilt hung in the room whenever Justin and I were together. It just seemed like we could have done something. Maybe we should have gone to him when he told us his neighbor was giving him problems. Maybe we should have convinced him to move. Our minds and hearts held on to a dozen different scenarios that were nothing more than wisps of smoke we could never really grab on to.

"We'll be going to Montana on Tuesday for the trial," Mom said, sitting down at the table beside us.

"And what happens then?" My brother's voice was short and curt.

"What do you think happens?" I asked, rolling my eyes at him.

"You think you know it all? What's your deal?"

"MY deal? You've been yelling at everyone for days. For weeks."

"Ohhh, my bad. Sorry my father was murdered and I can't manage to be nice to everyone all the time. My apologies. I'll try being more like you."

Mom's voice cut in sharply. "I don't know. But I know we have to stick together. We'll meet up with your aunt first and go from there. Above all, we need to rely on the Lord to give us strength."

The first time I walked into the courtroom in Montana, I felt like I was walking into a church. It had these big, beautiful wooden doors that opened up into a room with a split aisle. My family would sit on one side and the family of the defendant on the other. One praying for vindication and justice, and one hoping for a sentence kinder than what *we* certainly thought he deserved. The district attorney had invited us all to meet with him in the courtroom the day before the trial. He encouraged us to stay calm and collected. He said that was the best way to behave and that we should just let the facts and evidence speak for itself.

"Because of the way Mr. Perkins was murdered, there are going to be some really gruesome photographs displayed and included in evidence. It will be necessary that the jury see the way your son, brother, husband, father was shot — and how the bullet severed his spine." My aunt began to whimper.

"I apologize for my coarseness. And please know that at any point, you do not have to continue watching the proceedings if you do not wish to see this portion of the trial."

"Mr. Glencliff, how long do you expect the trial to go on?" I recognized Mom's voice from behind my shoulder.

"I expect that the trial could get drawn out to the full amount of allotted time, which would be 10 days. So, you'll need to prepare yourselves for that possibility." He paused and looked around the room, lowering his chin and averting his eyes.

"I'll leave you all to be together. I'm so very sorry for your loss, and if I can answer any more of your questions, please feel free to contact me. Otherwise, I'll see you in the morning." He shut the door behind him.

I sat down on a chair, reflecting on the way that the attorney had described Dad's death. *Gruesome.* I looked around the room. There was such unrest amongst my family. Bickering. Crying. Exhaustion. My aunt's voice piped up from across the table.

"Well, I hope the man gets what he deserves. And if he doesn't, you better believe they'll have to deal with me."

"He deserves to rot in prison," another relative echoed from the corner of the room.

"He's nothing but a son of a you-know-what," my uncle chimed in.

The Verdict

It was all becoming too much. I loosened my necktie and looked over at my brother and sister. We had known Dad's family would have a difficult time dealing with the murder trial. And rightfully so. I sat there, letting their words soak in.

What do I want for the man who killed my father? But more importantly, what does God want?

I let an easy sort of feeling wash over me as I tuned out the voices of my family members.

Lord, I am angry. I am hurt, and I don't understand how you could let Dad die like this. But, God, I know that nothing else is going to help me get through this. God, help me show my family that bitterness and hurt will only eat away their insides.

శ్రీశ్రీశ్రీ

The Lord is in control. This was the first thing that entered my mind as I woke up that morning, knowing that the proceedings would begin in only a few short hours. My stomach felt empty and nauseous. I jumped out of the bed and into the shower, anxious for it all to be over.

My family's temperament hadn't changed since the night before. They were angry and vindictive and had never experienced the freedom that came from truly forgiving someone. Honestly, I didn't, either. But something inside of me told me that if I didn't somehow figure out how, I'd be eaten up with hatred for the rest of my life. We piled out of our cars and walked briskly through the front doors of the courthouse. The women were all dressed in nice slacks or dresses, and the rest of us had done our best to press our dress shirts and pants. My sister Leslie moved beside me as we walked up the front stairs.

"What are we going to say, Larkin? If they ask me anything, I don't know what I'll say."

"It'll be okay, Les." I squeezed her hand. Inside, I was wondering if it would.

We sat, our bodies smashed against one another like sardines in a small can, on a row of wooden benches on the right side of the room. I noticed people on the other side of the aisle, also sitting in small groups. *They look just like us,* I thought to myself. *Except their loved one is the one that murdered Dad.* I looked over at Mom, sitting still and looking ahead toward the podium where the judge would reside. *She's probably praying,* I thought to myself. The judge entered in his traditional robes, and we all stood. It was time to begin.

కొంకొంకొ

It took three days to complete jury selection. It was a long, drawn-out process, and each day felt like it would never end. On the fourth day, the actual trial began. We'd arrive at the courthouse at 8 a.m. and would normally not leave until 8 p.m. — long after Montana's orange sun had buried itself below the horizon.

Each day brought new evidence. New testimonies and defense. And it seemed so interesting to me — that so much time went into both prosecuting and defending a person for a crime. I had never really been interested in the law, but despite the daily anxiousness I felt, I was grateful that the process was so thorough and involved.

On the eighth day, the trial concluded. The judge sent the jury members away to make their decision, and we all knew we wouldn't be able to breathe easily until they announced their verdict. We made our way out of the courthouse and to a restaurant to eat dinner. Though the question of what would happen hung heavily in all of our minds, we were able to relax with one another, knowing that the mental exhaustion we were all feeling would soon be over. After our meals had been devoured, I looked at everyone around me.

"Can I pray for us, you guys? Pray that whatever needs to happen will happen?"

Though I knew not all of my extended family members believed in Jesus, they allowed me to pray for the pending situation and that forgiveness and peace would flood through us.

Shortly after 11 p.m., we received a call alerting us that the jury had made a decision. "You have 15 minutes to get to the courthouse to hear the verdict," the man who telephoned informed us. It was a mad dash of grabbing coats and collecting bags. We piled into cars and somehow even managed to pick up Mom, who was stranded with a flat tire. It was a blur of moving parts and people, all anxious to arrive in time to hear the results of the proceedings.

Once in the courtroom, we all sat down in our familiar rows. The defendant was brought in — his eyes appearing empty. He averted his eyes from our gaze. The jury members filed in, one by one, and stood as the judge stood at his seat. He looked out on the small crowd of people that had gathered. It was approaching midnight.

"The jury has reached a verdict. The defendant is found guilty of deliberate homicide."

The words sent a warm sensation down my whole body, and I was enveloped in hugs and laughter and tears from my surrounding family. Leslie hugged me.

"Oh, I'm so glad. I'm so, so glad."

And so was I. But there was also a feeling I couldn't shake. A feeling that somehow, I needed to forgive the man standing 10 feet in front of me. That somehow, even though I didn't want to, I needed to show him what real love could look like.

༄༄༄

Months later, we sat in the county jail of our Michigan town. It had taken several months for the verdict to pass through various judicial channels, and after much time, Dad's murderer would receive his sentencing. It had been arranged that the sentencing be shown on a projector at our jailhouse, allowing us to both see the proceeding and speak, should we wish to share any final words.

The projection of the courtroom on the screen almost made me feel like I was there again. I could feel the hard wooden bench against my back and could almost taste the uncertainty and anger that had enveloped the room. On the screen, we saw the defendant. The judge sentenced him to life in prison and, upon doing so, asked if any of our family members would like to say anything to him before the sentencing ended.

Mom went first, the camera aimed toward her kind and gentle face. She talked about how he had been a good father to us kids. About how it was so sad that he would no longer be around to share in our future. My brother was next, followed by my sister. When my turn came, I stood, tears filling my eyes. As I began to speak, the defendant's eyes looked straight ahead at the screen.

"It pains me that I no longer have my dad. He will never get to see my children or teach them how to fish or see me grow older. But I know that Dad loved Jesus. And though it will never take away the stabbing and overwhelming realization that he isn't here with me anymore, it gives me a sense of relief knowing that he is resting in heaven with our Lord. And that one day we might join him." I paused, a lump forming in my throat. But I knew what I needed to say.

"If you don't know Jesus, I hope that during your time in prison, you find him in your heart. Because I want you to know that love. And I want you to know that I forgive you."

I sat back down, tears streaming down my cheeks. My heart felt lighter, and I could feel the anger and heaviness float away. And in that moment, all I could hear in my head was the voice of Dad. *I love you, kiddo.*

ৰ৵ৰ৵ৰ৵

If I could have my dad back, I would. I think that's pretty obvious. But there are so many things in this life we can't change. So, I keep working hard and loving my family and forgiving those who hurt me. I've seen what bitterness does to people who let it cling to them. Their eyes begin to look empty, and the words that slip off their tongue are like poison to their own spirits.

Dad's death taught me to love harder and let God's love fill me even more than I thought it could. I now know how to offer others empathy. How to serve my church family by telling my story.

The other day, Pastor Andy asked me to share my story with a group of men. It never gets easier to recall what happened to my family — to the father I loved with all of my heart. But it does get easier to recognize that God had a reason to allow me to forgive the man who killed my dad. And though I'll never see him again, I hope that somewhere in a Montana prison that man has found the love of Jesus. Because without it, we would all be a bunch of sinners sentenced to a life of pain.

Instead, we're given freedom and forgiveness. And that might be one of the most messed-up, crazy verdicts that was ever handed down.

ONE STEP AT A TIME
The Story of Katie
Written by Karen Koczwara

Oh, not again!

The sirens wailed behind me, and my heart skipped a beat. I sucked in my breath, clenching the steering wheel as I pulled to the side of the road.

Oh, man, I'm in trouble.

I've been down this road before — hauled off to jail and thrown in a cell.

Is this really happening to me again?

జ్ఞ జ్ఞ జ్ఞ

I was born on April 25, 1958 in Charlotte, Michigan. Two years before my arrival, my mother found herself pregnant during a relationship. She broke up with that man and met my father shortly after. They married, and she gave birth to a little girl, my older sister. Shortly after my birth, my parents discovered I had cerebral palsy, a condition affecting body movement. The doctors did not know if I would ever walk on my own.

My father carried me everywhere, and my parents often pushed me in a stroller when we went out. We attended church a couple times when I was very little, and my father gently carried me in and sat me down. I crawled from place to place, learning to get around on my hands and knees. From an early age, I remained strong-willed and stubborn, refusing to let my physical condition get me down.

When I turned 6, my parents got me braces for my ankles and legs, and I began walking on my own. At first, I took baby steps, but with each passing day, I got stronger. Within no time, I was able to run and play with the other kids. I never felt sorry for myself but instead considered my disability a gift.

My father worked for General Motors in Lansing, and my mother worked for a company called A & E, making aluminum refrigerator trim for appliances. We moved into a new home, which included a large yard. My sister and I enjoyed endless games of hide and seek, dodge ball and tag with the neighbor kids. At night, we settled into our own rooms upstairs — me in the larger room, and my sister in the smaller one. Like most siblings, we endured our share of squabbles. My sister acted out sometimes, convinced I was spoiled and getting more attention because of my special needs.

For the most part, ours was a happy home. My mother made a spectacular meatloaf, which I always devoured. Her homemade macaroni and cheese and spaghetti became two of my favorite dishes as well. My mother mastered the concept of multi-tasking, reading a book, eating popcorn and watching TV all at the same time. I watched her juggle everything, intrigued. She always burnt the popcorn just a bit, which I didn't mind at all.

Sometimes, we engaged in a family game of Monopoly, but I spent much of my time alone, playing with my dolls in my room. One of my battery-operated dolls actually walked, which I liked. My Easy-Bake Oven remained another childhood favorite.

Spending time with my grandparents brought me great joy, too. My grandmother often rocked me to sleep, and I cherished her tender arms around me. I sometimes sat in her lap, twirling her wedding ring around her finger. I spent ample time at my grandparents' house. They lived on a lake, and when my parents worked long hours, I spent my time exploring the landscape. The lake was my favorite place to be. I dangled my feet in the cool water and splashed in it, sometimes catching frogs. My grandfather taught me how to fish with cane poles instead of reels, and I caught on quickly. Once, he caught a turtle, and we both yelped with excitement when he pulled it from the water.

While my home life brought solitude and happiness, school proved a bit less peaceful. I loved learning, but I did not love the bullying I endured. Sometimes, on the playground, I caught kids making fun of me, imitating my walk. I went home in tears. I did not resent my disability, so why couldn't they just accept me as I was?

By junior high, I learned to give kids dirty looks when they stared at me or made fun of my condition. *Don't mess with me,* I said with my glaring eyes. *Just leave me alone.*

My sister moved out of the house at 16, leaving just me

at home with my parents. When I turned 17, I started hanging out with a new group of friends. They introduced me to pot, cigarettes and alcohol, and I experimented with them all. I liked the way the booze and pot made me feel — relaxed, happy and carefree. I began buying bags of pot, hiding it from my parents when I got home. I drank any cheap form of alcohol I could get my hands on — Mad Dog, beer, wine coolers, Bloody Marys and other cocktails. Velvet and Coke became a fast favorite. My older friends bought the drinks for us at the liquor store.

I began driving that same year, and soon after that, I landed my first job as a dishwasher at a local bar. I liked the work okay, but I liked the paycheck even better. It provided me with gas money, as well as a way to fund my cigarette and alcohol habit. I kept up my partying ways, going out with friends and looking to have a good time.

I graduated from high school, and my father helped me get a job at General Motors. My first assignment entailed ripping tickets off the printer and putting them on various parts in sequential order. My friend landed the same job, and I enjoyed working with her. I was able to sit down during my work, which worked out well with my cerebral palsy.

Not long after I began work at GM, the doctors diagnosed my mother with breast cancer. The news came as a shock to all of us. My mother spent the next two years battling the disease. She went through chemotherapy and lost all her hair. The doctors then performed a mastectomy and removed her breast. I watched my once-vibrant mother transform into a frail, sickly woman, and it saddened me. But I was too consumed with my own life, partying and working to spend much time with her at home. She passed away when I was 23.

My father grieved especially hard. He and my mother had enjoyed a wonderful marriage, almost making it to the 25-year mark. I knew he would be lonely without her. I lived at home for a while after she died and then moved out on my own. Five years later, the only grandmother I'd ever known passed away after battling stomach cancer for a year. After her death, my father gave me a little velvet pouch, which had her wedding ring inside. I pulled it out, remembering the many times I'd twirled it around her finger when I was a child. The ring had worn so thin that she had taped it on the bottom so it would not break. I assumed she'd never taken it off until she died. I would miss both her and my mother and the many special times we'd shared together.

Life marched on. In 1987, when I was 29, I went out on a Friday night after work. I stopped at a bar, and as usual, I left high and drunk. As I headed down the road, feeling good, I suddenly heard sirens behind me. I glanced behind me and saw an unmarked car on my tail. *Is this some sort of joke?* I wondered.

I pulled to the side of the road, and a cop walked over to the window. "Can I ask you to step out of the car?" he barked.

I did as he instructed, no longer feeling so good. Even in my high state of mind, I knew I might be in big trouble.

The cop issued a sobriety test, which I failed. "I'm going to need you to come with me," he said. He arrested me and hauled me off to jail.

My heart thudded a bit in my chest as I slumped in the back seat of his car. Still high, the severity of the situation did not fully hit me. But I began to feel scared as we pulled up to the police station. *Am I really going to jail? Is this really happening to me right now?*

I spent the night in the drunk tank, a humiliating experience. Someone offered me a thin mattress to throw on top of the hard slab that made up the bed in my cell. I crawled onto it, cold, miserable and humiliated. *I can't believe this. An hour ago, I was having the time of my life at the bar, and now I'm locked up in a dirty jail cell.*

The police gave me one phone call, and I chose to call my father.

"I, um, got arrested for drinking and driving," I said, nervously spitting out the words.

My dad was not happy about the situation and threw me a disgusted look when he came to pick me up. He gave me the silent treatment when I got home. I knew I had been irresponsible, and I did not blame him for getting angry with me. I was a grown woman now — old enough to know better.

After being slapped with a DUI and six months' probation, I began attending the required Alcoholics Anonymous meetings. I sat around with other alcoholics, and we swapped stories and talked about ways to hold ourselves accountable. I knew I needed to start making better choices in my life. If I didn't, I might face something even more serious next time and really hurt myself or the ones I loved. Plus, I was sick and tired of always being sick and tired, hung over after one too many nights of partying. It was time to start fresh.

I found a new group of friends and tried to clean up my life. For a while, it worked. I kept up my job, and two years after getting my DUI, I moved out of my father's house and into a place of my own. For a while, I kept on the straight path, but eventually, I fell back into my partying ways.

One night, I hung out at a bar, mingling with all the locals. Everyone, it seemed, knew my name. I ran into some girls, and they told me about a party put on by a local guy.

"Hey, he's my neighbor!" I said. I knew the guy had won the lottery a few years before. *Must be some party he's throwing.*

"Can you give us a ride over there?" the girls asked.

"Sure," I replied.

Not long after heading down the road, I heard the familiar roar of sirens behind me. *Oh, no. Not again.* My chest tightened, and I pulled to the side of the road.

I failed the sobriety test, and the cops hauled me off to jail. They slapped me with a second DUI. This time, instead of calling my father, I chose to phone my brother-in-law instead. Fear gripped me, as I realized the severity of what I'd done. Before attending my court hearing, I went back to Alcoholics Anonymous classes on my own. I made a decision to stop drinking and doing drugs, to get clean once and for all.

The judge was not happy to see me again. She assigned me two years' probation this time. "You need to report to the officer once a month with signed papers, verifying you are attending AA meetings. Is this clear?" she said.

I nodded and hung my head. *I've got to stick to this. I can't keep living like this. My poor decisions have already cost me in money, time and relationships. I need to stay sober and stay on track so I never have to show up in this courtroom again.*

I enjoyed attending the AA meetings. The leaders discussed a higher power and a creator. Some believed this higher power was God, while others chose to believe in something else. I chose to say God, though I really hadn't given much thought to him in years. Unlike my first time in AA, I decided to get a sponsor this time. My female sponsor met with me on a regular basis and encouraged me on my path toward sobriety. Having been sober for several years herself, she knew a great deal about the AA program and believed in it. I did what she said, following her suggestions and advice. *This time is going to be different,* I told myself, determined. *I am not going back to my old ways. I'm going to stay out of the bars and clean up my life.*

In 1995, my friend Daryl invited me to church with him. "You gotta check out this church, Katie," he said. "I think you will really like it."

I hadn't thought about church in years. In fact, I

hadn't been since I was a little girl, when my father had carried me through those church doors. "Sure, why not? I'll try it," I agreed.

I began attending church with Daryl and his wife, June (who quickly became one of my best friends), and just as he'd said, I really liked it. The people were very warm and welcoming, and the pastor spoke enthusiastically as he read from the Bible. I knew a little about the Bible, but the pastor explained everything in a clear and concise manner. I threw myself into Bible studies and prayer meetings, suddenly unable to get enough.

The pastor described God as a loving being who had created us because he wanted a relationship with us. He'd sent his son, Jesus, to earth to die on the cross for our sins — the wrong things we'd done. None of us, no matter how good we felt about ourselves, could get to heaven on our own, he said. We needed a Savior to forgive us of our sins, and that Savior was Jesus.

By inviting him into our lives, we could enjoy a relationship with him that would last for eternity. This did not mean we would not face struggles on this earth. But when we encountered them, we would not face them alone. God was our rescuer, saving us from our pain and our sorrows. He offered joy, peace and hope, while the world offered self-gratification and disappointment.

This all just makes so much sense, I realized. *I see now that God has been the missing piece in my life.* I thought about the many nights I'd gone out partying with my friends, the smoke curling around my lips as I took a hit of a joint. I'd been looking for happiness in all the wrong places, hoping to find fulfillment in drinking and getting high. But in the morning, I'd only wound up alone, empty, hung over and depressed. Instead of seeking out God, I'd just kept doing the same thing, but I'd only experienced the same results. After two DUIs, I'd come to the end of myself. I was tired of not feeling good, tired of being lonely, tired of finding superficial friendships in bars and nightclubs. I needed Jesus in my life. Only he could truly fill the emptiness in my heart.

One night, I went to bed and lay there, thinking about Jesus. The simple but beautiful message of his love and forgiveness resonated with me. I felt excited realizing someone loved me unconditionally. Right then and there in the stillness of my room, I invited him into my life.

God, I prayed, *I know I need you. I've tried doing things my way for a long time, but it hasn't worked out very well. The pastor says we need a Savior, and I know that Savior is you. Please come into my heart. I want to know you and to live for you from this moment on.*

The next night, unsure God had heard my prayer, I prayed again — just in case. I felt a wonderful warmth, comfort and peace seep into my heart. I knew I had made the right decision, perhaps the best decision of my entire life.

I did not tell anyone about my prayer. But two weeks later, I approached my pastor and told him what I'd done. "A couple weeks ago, I made a decision to invite Jesus into my heart," I said.

"That is wonderful!" he congratulated me. "Why didn't you tell anyone sooner?"

I shrugged and laughed. "I guess I just didn't think to."

My pastor and I talked, and I realized I did not need to pray more than once to ask God into my heart. There was no right or wrong way to become a Christian. The important thing was my heart, he said. I had made a sincere decision to follow Jesus, and God had heard my earnest prayer. I now had the Holy Spirit, God's unseen spiritual helper, to guide me through life. The Holy Spirit would gently nudge me and help navigate me through life. The Holy Spirit would remind me when I'd done something wrong and help keep me on the right path. I had the power of the Holy Spirit in my heart now, and no one could take that away.

I began reading my Bible, memorizing as many scriptures as possible. Philippians 4:13 became a favorite: "I can do all things through Christ who strengthens me." I thought about the physical challenges I'd encountered over the years and how I'd never allowed them to get me down. *I now realize it was you giving me the strength, God. You are the one who has helped me to walk. You are also the one who gave me strength to become sober. Thank you for watching over me even before I knew you.*

My pastor gave permission for us to start holding AA meetings in the basement at the church. I began attending the meetings, along with several other church members recovering from alcoholism. Outsiders who did not attend the church came as well.

I thanked God for the opportunity to reach out to the community. While I highly believed in AA, I also knew that it was ultimately God who helped us achieve our goals. As my favorite Bible verse indicated, in him, we could do all things.

That same year, I met a guy named Brad at church. He approached me one day and asked me on a date. With his hazel eyes and sturdy build, I found him very handsome. I had never noticed him before, but, flattered, I accepted his invitation. We went to dinner and had a nice time chatting and getting to know one another. He told me about his career, and I told him about mine at GM. I learned Brad was best friends with our pastor. He was easy to talk to and easy on the eyes as well. We began dating, and our relationship progressed quickly.

The experience was new for me. In the past, I had always looked for men at the bar. But those relationships were superficial, and I'd always wound up disappointed. Now that I had God in my life, I knew it was important to marry a man who shared my beliefs. Brad had a strong faith in God, and it showed. He treated others with respect and was especially active at church. *This is the sort of man I should be with,* I told myself.

Though I had come far in life despite my disability, my cerebral palsy still created challenges sometimes. During one of my first dates with Brad, I tripped and fell and hurt my toes. The injury required surgery.

During my recovery, June became my daytime caretaker, coming over to my house and carefully dressing my wounds. She helped me with my right leg brace as I became steady on my feet again.

Brad would come over after work, spending the evening and cooking for me. I really appreciated his attentiveness to me. God continued to nudge my heart. *This is the man I have for you.*

On Valentine's Day in 1997, Brad took me to a nice dinner in nearby Lansing. On our way back to Charlotte, he said, "I forgot something at the church. I just need to run by there real quick."

Brad had a set of keys to the church, as he was very involved in ministry there. I followed him into the building, and he walked toward the altar. "Sit down there for a minute," he instructed, motioning toward the front row seats.

I did as he asked, not sure what he was up to. Moments later, Brad dropped to his knee and pulled out a ring.

"Will you marry me, Katie?" he asked, grinning.

I stared at him, shocked and elated. "Yes!" I cried happily.

Brad and I began eagerly planning our wedding. He owned a house in town, but it had a curved staircase, which I knew might be very difficult for me to climb. So I suggested we move into my place when we married.

In December 1998, my grandfather passed away. I grieved him, just as I had my grandmother. We'd enjoyed many happy memories together at the lake, and I would miss him very much. I thanked God for giving Brad the opportunity to get to know him as well. The two had developed a special bond before his death.

In July 1999, Brad and I married at the beautiful Frances Park in nearby Lansing. The warm summer sun shone down on us as we exchanged vows in the rose garden. I wore a gorgeous dress, which included a nearly 5-pound train.

We extended an open invitation to all our friends and family, and many people from church showed up to support us. We kept the ceremony short and simple and enjoyed a special reception afterward. It was a lovely day in every way, and I thanked God for bringing me such a wonderful partner in Brad. After stepping away from the bar scene, I was not sure where I'd meet my future husband. But God had saved a very special man for me, and he could not have been more perfect for me. It was time to begin the next chapter of our lives.

☙☙☙

The church Brad and I attended closed, and we began attending Real Life Church in Charlotte. The church was full of many young people, but folks of any age were welcome. The worship was great, and the pastor gave a great message each week. Real Life lived up to its name. We found it to be a church full of people living real life, flaws, bumps and all. They really loved God and knew how to love others. I was so happy to have a place to call home.

Since marrying Brad, life has not been a perfectly smooth road. In March 2006, Brad underwent a quadruple bypass. I was quite scared when I learned the news, but I sensed in my heart that God, in his kind, gentle way, assured me my husband would be just fine. Indeed, he was.

In 2008, the economy took a turn for the worse, and GM laid me off. I have not returned to work since. Brad continued to work, and God continued to provide all our needs.

One day, five years ago, I went to get up out of my chair, and I fell. I immediately heard a bone snap, and the searing pain came seconds later. I went to the doctor and learned I'd broken a bone in my shoulder and injured my rotator cuff. I underwent a couple surgeries to repair the damage. I also had trouble with my right knee and underwent cartilage repair. The physical therapy didn't go very well, and I have struggled physically since. Cerebral palsy will always provide certain challenges for me, but even to this day, I still consider it a gift from God. I continue to take one day at a time, doing the best I can, thanking God for the life he's given me.

James 1:2 remains one of my favorite Bible verses: "Consider it pure joy, my brothers and sisters, whenever you face trials of many kinds." Some might think it strange to consider trials a joy, but I look at them as a blessing. They draw us closer to God and remind us of his unfailing love. In the end, we come out stronger and closer to him.

As I think back on my early years, it's hard to imagine there was a time when I did not have church or God in my life. I tried doing things my way for many years, looking for love, acceptance and fulfillment in drugs, alcohol and bars. But while those things offered a temporary escape from my problems, they always left me feeling empty inside.

Today, I find fulfillment in Jesus Christ alone. He is my maker, my confidant and my best friend. Even on my weakest days, I find strength in him. Together, we walk through life, one step at a time.

GUARDED
The Story of Bridget
Written by Arlene Showalter

"Bridget, I have some bad news," Jax said. Jax was the brother of my boyfriend, Tex. "Please, sit down."

My heart pounded as I clutched the phone with whitened knuckles. "Okay. What is it?"

"Tex is dead."

What? How can he be dead? We were together just two days ago.

"Bridget, are you there? Did you hear what I said?"

"Yes," I choked. "I'm just trying to wrap my head around it. What happened? When? Where?"

"He was driving home …"

"He's not supposed to drive," I replied. "Because his license is suspended."

"When did Tex ever follow the rules? He was driving home …"

"Was he drunk?"

"Yes. He drove the truck into the pond."

I pushed the *end call* button, shocked and distraught over Tex's death. *Maybe it's time to get my own life on track.*

❧❧❧

OUT OF THESE ASHES

"I'm not going to tell her. You have to," I heard Mom say to Dad as I watched TV in the basement where I shared a bedroom with my younger sister Megan.

A few moments later, he descended halfway down the basement steps and halted. Then he turned and went back upstairs.

That was weird, I thought briefly before going back to my show.

"Where's Dad?" I asked the next day as dinnertime approached.

"He left," Mom said.

"For where?"

"He left *us,*" Mom said. "He told me he wants a divorce. Didn't he tell you when he went downstairs last night?"

"He never said a word. He came halfway down and then went back upstairs."

Dad wants a divorce? He doesn't love Mom anymore? He doesn't love his kids anymore? I lay alone in my bed that night, confused and fearful thoughts creating a tangled mass of confusion in my head. *How could I not see this coming? I'm 13.* I flopped on my stomach and punched the pillow, squirming in search of a more comfortable position to snatch some elusive sleep.

I should've been able to pick up on something. I squeezed my eyes closed and pressed the pillow against my face and around my ears to block out Megan's even breathing. *I guess she's too young to realize what divorce really means.*

Dad, a successful attorney, expected his family to uphold an untarnished image to reflect his achievements. The tension in the home equaled that in a courtroom as he argued an important case. Only Mom's relaxed attitude on life and superb sense of humor gave us kids a semblance of balance.

Soon after Dad's sudden departure, both of Mom's parents died. They, like Mom, took life as it came, and they cared little of the opinions of others. Dad hadn't liked Mom's parents because they provided no burnish to his image, so our contact with them was limited.

After a stroke, Grandpa spent years in bed at home. When Grandma slipped away in her sleep, the shock hit Grandpa so hard his children had him hospitalized, where he died three days later.

Right after their deaths, I had a scary dream about my 10-years-older favorite cousin, Christopher. He always engaged my sister and me in tickle fights when he visited, and we adored him. In my dream, I saw him driving a truck. Suddenly zombies came out of the ground, and his truck crashed, killing him.

What was that all about? I struggled to breathe, and my heart thudded. *Is that an omen or a nightmare?*

The next day we got the news that Christopher had been shot and killed in California.

❧❧❧

"I'm moving to Texas," my best friend, Charlotte, told me while I was still reeling from Dad's abandonment and three deaths.

"I can't bear it," I sobbed to Mom later. "First, Dad leaves. Then Grandma and Grandpa die. Then Christopher's murdered. She's my best friend. Can I go with her?"

Mom's eyes filled with tears. She struggled with the same losses.

"We already talked to Charlotte's mom, and she's okay with it. She thinks it would be good for Charlotte to already have a friend when she goes to a new school."

"If you insist," Mom said. Her voice wavered. "It breaks my heart to see you go, but I understand, and I'll let you if that is what you really want."

"It is. Thanks, Mom."

❧❧❧

I moved to Texas with Charlotte's family. Her mom visited the local school to enroll us both.

"You have to have legal guardianship to enroll Bridget."

"I don't think that will be a problem."

"Both parents have to agree — in writing."

"Dad, I'm down here in Texas with Charlotte." I called when we got back to the house. "Her parents have to have legal guardianship for me to attend school here."

"What are you doing down there?" he roared.

"Why should you care *where* I am?" I asked. "You never call or visit, so what's it to you?"

"Your mother is okay with releasing her rights for your harebrained actions?"

"She let me come because I wanted to. She cared about me enough to let me come."

"Well, I'm not going to be responsible for you if you can't be responsible." Dad signed away all his rights as a parent, legally disowning me to remove all financial responsibility for me.

I buried the hurt and moved on with my life. I enjoyed the fresh start in Texas. Back home in Michigan, some cruel kids had started false rumors about me sleeping around. The gossip took on a life of its own, and I couldn't deal with the lies. Nobody knew those ugly words in my new school.

After a wonderful year in Texas, Charlotte's parents split up. Her father decided to return to Michigan, and Charlotte chose to go with him. I had little choice but to return myself.

Mom had to go to work when Dad left and only qualified for a minimum-wage job. Neither of my elder siblings seemed tuned in to her financial struggles. When I returned, I got my own job and started helping her by paying bills and buying groceries. As soon as I qualified for a driver's license, I helped her with errands.

The struggle built a bond between us that grew stronger with each year.

"Why did Dad leave?" I asked.

"He'd been cheating on me," Mom said. "Your brother caught him on a scouting trip."

"Cheating? Dad?"

"Yes. That's why your brother has been going to therapy. To get over the shock."

∾∾∾

Dad remarried the week of the divorce, further rocking my world. Next, Dad demanded that Mom buy out his half of the interest in our home. Unable to do so, we put the house on the market.

"What will we do with our cats?" I asked Mom when the house sold.

"We have no choice but to take them to the shelter," she said. "I found an apartment for us, but pets are not allowed. I'm so sorry, Bridget."

I loaded up our cats and drove to the animal shelter alone, constantly blinking back tears that threatened to obscure my vision.

He doesn't care what happens to any of us. He doesn't care how much he's hurting us with his own selfish actions. He ranted about me being irresponsible when I went to Texas. How irresponsible is he? Dumping Mom and us without a care of how we will eat or where we will live.

I tried to block the cats' pitiful mewing as I hugged each goodbye. Anger clogged my heartbreak.

I hate him for doing this to us.

Even though we were crowded in the apartment and working minimum wage, Mom reveled in a freedom she'd never experienced under Dad's condemning eye. She relaxed, and we relaxed with her.

Mom involved herself in her children's lives. I loved photography, so Mom accompanied me on my photo shoots. We discussed photos, angles and composition as we discussed ways for me to improve. Our friendship developed along with my art.

After high school graduation, I turned into a know-it-all and started driving Mom nuts with my attitude and condescension.

"You are acting just like your father!" she said, wringing out a dishcloth at the kitchen sink. "Maybe you should go live with him if you are as smart as he is."

"Fine! That's just what I'll do." I jumped up and flounced out of the room.

Dad and his wife, Mona, lived right around the corner. Amazingly, he agreed to let me move in. Soon after that, Mom went to live near Megan, who'd moved to Arizona.

After Dad left, Mom lived like a free spirit. Our friends could drift over anytime they pleased. We had no curfew. Mom wanted us to explore our creativity and gave little or no parameters to her children.

But Dad had rules. Lots of rules. No friends allowed. No talking late on the phone. I had to account for my whereabouts at all times. *I'm a legal adult, and he treats me like a child. I wish I'd kept my mouth shut and stayed with Mom. Maybe she wouldn't have moved away if I had treated her better.*

I started cosmetology school at Mona's suggestion and also got a job at the local steakhouse.

"Hey, I'm Jake." My co-worker grinned.

"Hi, I'm Bridget."

We talked some when business was slow, but when Jake asked me on a date, I hesitated. *Do I want any sort of commitment? Look how my parents ended up. Is it worth the risk to end up with a guy who's going to verbally bash me like Dad did with Mom?*

ॐॐॐ

"You want to come to my apartment?" Jake asked, two years into our dating relationship.

"Sure." *Wow, this guy really likes me. He's finally inviting me to his place.*

He drove me to his seedy neighborhood and let me in.

"How about spending the night with me?" *He must really like me because he's asking me to stay over.*

"I can't be." I stared at the pregnancy test in my hand. Plus. Positive. Yes. "Sex one time, and now I'm pregnant?"

I took several more tests and then pondered my options. *I'm unmarried. No career. Jake's a cool guy, but he's also a pothead loser. There's no way I can be tied to him for life. No way.*

I called an abortion clinic in another town and set up an appointment. My car died the same day as the scheduled date.

"Daisy, I need help." I called my oldest sister.

"What's the matter?"

"I got myself knocked up and have to get rid of it. Long story. Loser dad." I drew a deep breath. "You know I can't tell Dad about this. He'd kill me. Will you drive me to the clinic?"

"Of course. What are sisters for?"

"What's this I hear about an abortion?" Dad yelled a few days later.

"What abortion? What are you talking about?"

"Don't play stupid with me. Daisy told me all about it."

I groaned. She and I had had an argument the following day. *So, ratting me out to Dad is her way of getting even. Now I know what sisters are really for.*

"It's true." *It's useless to argue against a seasoned attorney. He'll dig the truth out of me sooner or later.*

"How could you be so dumb? If you can't act like a responsible adult, then I am going to have to treat you like an irresponsible child." He held out one hand and scowled. "Give me your house key. Furthermore," he continued, assuming a lawyer stance, "you will have a curfew, and I expect you to be in the house by then. Otherwise, you are out on the street."

I retaliated by modeling Dad's own behavior. If very displeased, he shut his mouth — sometimes for days at a

Out Of These Ashes

time — and glared. I gave him the "big freeze," and he returned it. We walked in sullen silence for days.

"Will you go talk to your daughter?" Mona yelled. "This silence is ridiculous, and it's killing me."

❧❧❧

"It's just too hot out there," Mom said when she returned to Michigan. Then a mutual friend introduced me to Tex. *Another pothead, drunken guy that would surely turn Dad's stomach.* I gladly said yes when he asked for a date.

Tex had lost his license because of drinking, but he often drove the three miles from his home to where his parents lived. We dated nine months before I got the call from his brother.

"Bridget, Tex was killed tonight."

"*What?*" I clutched my phone tighter. "How?"

"You know how he'd drive, even though he wasn't supposed to?"

"Yeah."

"Tonight he missed a curve when he was driving home. Just as he headed toward the pond, he crashed and got ejected. His head hit a rock, and that's what killed him."

I laid my phone down, deep in shock. Then I called my mom.

"My life is over," I wailed.

"Why? Tell me what happened, Bridget."

"Tex was killed tonight. He crashed his truck."

"I'll be right over."

I'm all alone again. I stared into the black night. *Will I never have anyone who loves me and will stay with me?*

దేదేదే

Maybe I need to get back to church. Tex's death reminded me of how fragile life could be.

I recalled a vision of Jesus I had when I was only 5. While playing at the edge of our driveway, a cloud floated down and hovered inches from the pavement. Jesus and two other men stood on the cloud. He smiled at me. I no longer remembered what he'd said, but I knew I felt safe and loved.

Then, when I was 9, I began going to Bible studies a neighbor lady held in her home. I loved doing the lessons, which she mailed out for us. They came back, corrected and littered with shining stickers for good work done. I loved those stickers and worked hard at my lessons.

"I am going to talk to each one of you individually," Miss Peters said one night. "If you want to accept Jesus into your life and heart, I will pray with you."

"Do you want Jesus in your life?" she asked when my turn came and we sat alone in the kitchen.

"Yes, I do."

"I'm so happy to hear that, Bridget. Let's do that right now. Just pray after me."

"Jesus, I thank you for dying on the cross for me. I am

sorry for all my sins, and I want you to live in my heart and guide my life from now on. Amen."

After Tex's death, I wanted to return to the Jesus I knew as a child. I found a church with a pastor who had a passion for teaching. But, while I drank in his messages, I also developed a taste for alcohol, even though I'd dated drunks and hated how it had affected them. *Maybe I need to find out its attraction for myself.*

I drank more and more while going to the church and learning more and more about Jesus.

"Your life isn't a random act," the pastor said one Sunday. "Each person here was born for a specific purpose in life. Everyone here has value."

৵৵৵

"I have to stop," I told God one night, alone in my bathroom. "My own drinking is getting out of hand, and I saw firsthand what it did to Jake and Tex and others that I know. But now I'm hooked on it, too." I stared into the mirror and frowned at my own reflection.

"I can't do this on my own anymore, God. I need your help to overcome the compulsion to drink. I want to follow you 100 percent and discover your purpose for me."

A friend at church told me about Smile FM, a local Christian station on the radio. The music made me love him more, and the messages helped me understand him more. Finally, I yielded all of my life to Jesus. *I want to find the purpose you have for me on the earth and live it out.*

I earned enough money to buy a large trailer when I was 27 and asked Mom to move in with me. It had a huge kitchen, and we spent many hours together, baking, discussing life and growing closer.

❧❧❧

"You and Bill should go out together," Daisy said five years after Mom and I moved into the trailer.

"He's your friend, not mine." I'd known Bill since I was 13.

"He's a good guy, and I think he's interested in you."

"Don't think so." *No way am I going out with my sister's friend. Besides, he's a jock, and jocks don't appeal to me.*

Then, Daisy and I spotted Bill at our local yearly carnival.

"You should go out with him," she whispered, elbowing me as he approached.

"Totally not interested in jocks," I muttered.

"He's got a big heart. You're selling yourself short."

"Hi, Daisy. Bridget." Bill approached with a wide grin. "Nice to see you ladies."

I stepped back with a slight frown. *Not encouraging this dude. Not at all.*

"You're a jerk," Daisy said later. "Someday you'll regret not giving Bill a chance."

"Bill asked for your phone number," Daisy told me a little while later.

"And?" Annoyance crept into my voice.

"I gave it to him."

"Why did you do that? You know how I feel about him."

"Just give him *one* chance," she begged. "At the very least, be polite when he calls."

"Since you put me into this position, I'll try."

"Hello." I tried to keep my tone friendly when Bill called.

"Would you consider going out with me?" he asked.

I was quite pleasantly surprised with how genuine Bill was on the phone and discovered we had many things in common, so I decided to give him one chance. "Yeah, I guess."

"How about that nice Irish restaurant in town? We can go to the comedy club afterward."

"Well, okay."

"Good! I'll pick you up at 7 on Friday. Does that work for you?"

We went to the Irish restaurant. Afterward, we went to the comedy club. I was walking several steps ahead of him.

If you can't keep up, then I don't want to be with you, I thought, annoyed at his slow pace.

Later, Bill told me, "I could tell you were a little put out, but I figured I'd get there when I got there." He grinned.

What? This guy isn't buying any of my crap. Maybe I should give him a second thought.

సానిసాని

Bill won my heart with his unfailing kindness and loyalty, plus we shared a passion for ice cream. He accepted that I was a "package deal" and treated both Mom and me with unfailing kindness.

I moved in with Bill after four years of serious dating, while Mom stayed in our trailer. I also started looking for a new church home around the same time.

"Do you know where Emily goes to church now?" I asked my friend Georgia. We both knew her from the time she and her husband, Pastor Andy, completed an internship at my old church. I remembered how genuine they both had been in their interactions with the congregation.

"Yes. She and Pastor Andy go to Real Life over in Charlotte. You should go. I think you'd like it."

I went the first time, all alone, cautious and a little touchy that I'd be judged for shacking up. *I know it's wrong, and I'm quite sure they feel the same way, so maybe they'll reject me when they know I'm not living right.*

But a lady met me at the door with the sweetest smile. "Hello! Welcome to Real Life. Here is our bulletin. Please allow me to show you around."

We ran into Emily during the tour, and she came over. She welcomed me with arms spread wide.

"It's *so* good to see you," she said, hugging me hard. I squirmed a little. *Whoa. Crowding my personal space here.* I always preferred blending in and never felt comfortable with being noticed or singled out for any sort of attention. *Not sure I'm cool with this.*

"Would you like to sit with me during the service?" she asked.

"We are blessed to be a blessing," Pastor Andy said during his message. "God put us here for a reason. We have a real purpose in life. All good things come from God, and he blesses us to be a blessing."

I remembered what I'd learned at my first church. *I was born for a reason, and now Pastor Andy says we were born to bless others as we have been blessed.*

Bill is a real blessing. He accepts Mom and her health issues and helps in every way he can. Mom is a blessing. She's always let me be me. Always encouraged me. Always stood by me. And, God, you blessed me all those years when I ignored you. I want to come back here again and hear more of what Pastor Andy has to say.

ॐॐॐ

"Hold on. I'll be right back." Bill stood up on Christmas morning right after we'd opened our presents.

"Okay." *He must've left his cell phone in the bedroom.*

A few minutes later, our mammoth dog, Molly, stood in front of me just as Bill reappeared. She slung her tail in circles and slobbered all over me.

"Why are you in my face?" I gave her a gentle push.

"Molly has something for you."

"Molly? What, a doggie bone?" I reached out to push her again and saw something sparkly on her collar.

"What is this?" I plucked the paper and opened it.

Will you marry me? I read.

"Are you serious?" I jumped to my feet and threw my arms around a waiting Bill. "Wow, we're going to get *married*? Really? Yes, yes!"

My heart filled with joy as we visited our families that day and I showed off the proof of Bill's love and commitment to me.

❧❧❧

"Bridget, this is Bill's dad. He's been in a little accident." I answered the phone while shoveling snow from my brother's driveway.

Not another accident. Am I going to lose him like Tex? Please, God, no!

"How? Where? When?"

He gave me the directions, and I dashed to my car. "Why does it have to snow right now, God?" I cried as I inched my way toward the scene. Later, I learned that a kid had been texting and lost control of her car from the deep ruts in the road. A semi-driver swerved to avoid hitting her. Instead, he hit Bill head-on. He stopped his rig to check on Bill and called Bill's dad at the scene.

Deb, a former co-worker, had seen the accident and

threw a blanket over Bill's car to keep it as warm as possible while crews worked to release him.

"He's dead," I cried when I first saw the covered car. I called my friend Georgia.

"Please pray for Bill. He's been in a horrible accident, and the crews are trying to get him out right now. He can't die. God wouldn't bring a decent man into my life just to have him die."

Two Jaws of Life broke before the third finally released Bill from his metal prison two and a half hours later.

The doctors put Bill into a forced coma for four days. They put a rod in his femur, four pins in his foot and a plate in his pelvis. Pastor Andy and Emily came and prayed for him while he was still in the coma, committing his and my lives and futures to God.

He did not die.

When he finally came home, we split the day into three eight-hour blocks. His mom, dad and I each took a shift.

"I'm going to walk at our wedding," he promised. He concentrated hard on his physical therapy and fulfilled that promise — with the aid of a cane.

"I can't believe this is finally happening!" I said to Mom the day before the wedding. "I'm really getting *married*."

"Been a long, hard road, but here you are!" Mom hugged me hard. "I'm proud of you, Bridget. And you know how much I love Bill!"

The day before the ceremony, the girls of the family enjoyed a day of pampering, happy gossip and fun. Daisy and Megan joined Mom and me, along with Georgia, for manicures and pedicures. Later that evening, we enjoyed a fancy dinner before retiring at a lovely hotel.

The next day Bill and I married in a cozy ceremony at a bed and breakfast, pledging ourselves to one another and to God forever.

❧❧❧

"Mom has to go to the doctor today," I told Bill three months after our wedding. "I can't miss work. Do you think you could take her?"

"Of course. I'd be happy to. Your mom and I go way back, you know."

"I know." I laughed. "My mom has liked you since the first time Daisy invited you over to the house to hang out with her other friends."

"I need to talk to you." Mom called me at work.

"Okay." Something in her voice told me she had something serious to discuss, so I canceled all my evening appointments and drove over to her house.

Later, I looked at Mom across the table, looking pale and scared. "What did the doctor say?"

"I have lung cancer."

"Mom called me today," I told Bill when I got home. "You know why, don't you?"

"Yes. When I took your mom to see the doctor, she walked in with a firm step. But, when she came out, she was all droopy-like. I asked her, 'What's going on?' She said, 'I'm going to die.' She made me promise not to tell you. She wanted to do that herself."

"I guess I shouldn't be surprised. She's smoked like a chimney all her life." Tears filled my eyes. "I'm going to lose my best friend."

"I know." Bill gathered me into his arms for a long embrace. "I'm with you."

When Mom got depressed, Bill said, "You have two choices here. You can stay down, or you can *suck it up, Sally.*"

Mom, who'd known Bill since he was a young teen, had enjoyed a special relationship with him over the years, and now it paid off.

Mom grew sicker, and Bill jumped in and helped wherever he could.

"Let's suck it up, Sally," he'd tease as she puked her guts out.

She puffed out her thinning chest and grinned through the pain. But she had many questions about God and eternity I couldn't answer.

"Can you help me?" I asked Pastor Andy.

"Sure. I'll visit her tomorrow."

"I'd really appreciate that."

His generosity impressed me because I'd had little direct interaction with him up to that time.

"Why should I trust *him*," she asked me after his first

GUARDED

visit. "I don't know him. Why should I believe what he tells me?"

"Just give him time, Mom. I've been going to the church he pastors for a long time, and he's the real deal."

Andy's genuine concern won out, and Mom opened up to him. He visited her every day of her last hospital stay.

"I gave my life to Jesus today," Mom told me when I arrived for my daily visit to the hospital. "Pastor Andy guided me with prayer."

Mom's lungs gave out, and the doctor put her on life support after she slipped into a coma. A lady from hospice drew me to one side to discuss when and how to let Mom go.

"I can't do it," I said. "I won't do it. I want my mom to live."

"Here is her CAT scan," she said. "Look at her lungs. There is no room left for her to breathe." She paused and laid a hand on my arm. "She's dying, Bridget. Do you think she'd want to extend her life like this — continually hooked up to a breathing machine?"

I shook my head. "No. We've discussed this. She would hate it."

Later, Pastor Andy came in the room.

"I don't have the courage to do this," I said, looking at him. "I need your wisdom."

"Do you believe your mother has accepted Jesus into her life and heart?"

"Of course, I do."

"And you realize the moment she draws her last breath here on earth, she will open her eyes and see Jesus?"

"Yes." Tears formed and fell. "What am I supposed to do — just yank the plug and let her die?"

"I can't tell you what to do," he replied. "But you know God is with you every moment of every day. Only he can give you the wisdom and strength you need to make the right decision."

I thought about the breathing tech who'd come into Mom's room a few days prior. He'd asked, "Do you mind if I pray for your mom?"

I had nodded my okay, and he proceeded to ask God to saturate Mom in his peace.

"I have to let her go," I said to Pastor Andy. "It's what she wants. But," I paused. "She really wanted to get baptized before she died. I don't think that's possible now."

"Sure it is." Andy grabbed a bucket used for bed baths and put some warm water in it. He took Mom's limp hand and prayed with her, then he dipped his fingers in the warm water and daubed her face.

"God, what should I do?" I prayed later as I drove home. "Mom never wanted to be on life support." Tears dampened my cheeks. "But how can I let her go? She's been my best friend all my life."

Psalm 18:19 reads, "He brought me out into a spacious place. He rescued me because he delighted in me." The verse popped into my head as I stopped at a red light.

"Are you telling me that it's time for you to take Mom to a spacious place — heaven, God? You are rescuing her from cancer and delivering her into your presence?"

Comforting silence wrapped warm arms around my hurting heart. "And you are delighted in Mom. Jesus, thank you for your love. Your kindness. Your grace. Mom is the best mom you could've given me. Give me the strength to do the right thing and release her. Now I know that real life is just around the bend for her."

I authorized the staff to turn off the machines and released Mom into God's eternal care.

అఅఅ

I cried for weeks, crying out *to* God for strength and then *against* him in anger. "How could you let her die when I needed her so?"

Gradually I relaxed as I realized how much God loved me and cared about me. He brought me Bill when he knew I'd need him the most. The breathing tech came at the perfect time to pray and put my own heart at rest. Pastor Andy and Emily were like two faithful soldiers, never resting, always available when I needed them.

I allowed myself to move on in life and enjoy all God had given me.

అఅఅ

"Do you think we'll ever get pregnant?" I asked Bill as our third anniversary approached.

"Sometimes all we need is time," he said.

"Look at this," he said the next evening. "My co-worker showed me this ad from St. Vincent's. She was adopted from this organization and suggested we try the same route."

"I don't care *how* we get kids," I said. "I just want a family."

"Are you sure you're not just trying to fill the void of your mom's passing? That wouldn't be the right reason to do this."

"No. I want a family. Let's go through the foster care training and see what happens."

"I can live with that."

"We have a lovely baby boy we think would be perfect for the two of you," our new caseworker said.

We brought 4-month-old Matthew home as our first foster child and began the process for legal adoption.

Matthew filled our lives and home with coos and giggles, but nine months later, as I changed out of my work clothes, I winced as I removed my bra.

"Ouch! That hurt."

"My breast really hurts," I texted Megan.

"Go to the doctor, NOW!" she texted back.

I glanced at my watch. "Can't now. It's after 5 p.m. I will call first thing in the morning."

"Good. Keep me posted."

"We've run some tests," Dr. Rita said. "We don't think

it's anything, but thought we saw something on the scan. I want to do a biopsy to rule out anything abnormal."

After the biopsy, she said, "I'm pretty sure it's cancer. But I don't want you to panic, and don't read anything online. It'll just increase your anxiety. Bring your hubby to the office on your next visit."

On our next visit, she told me, "You have stage 3 cancer of the breast." Her warm eyes caught and held my own. "We will approach this calmly and methodically. Here is our battle plan."

"You can't die," Bill said on the way home. "I'm not raising a baby on my own."

"I'm not going to die," I replied. I couldn't imagine God would have blessed us with Matthew just to have me die and have him raised by a single dad. I loved God and did my best to trust him with my life.

When we got to the house, I picked up the Bible Mom and I read together in the hospital. I turned to Psalm 91 and found many lines that comforted and encouraged me.

"Whoever dwells in the shelter of the Most High will rest in the shadow of the Almighty."

"I will say of the LORD, 'He is my refuge and my fortress, my God, in whom I trust.'"

"He will cover you with his feathers, and under his wings you will find refuge."

"You will not fear the terror of night."

"A thousand may fall at your side, ten thousand at your right hand, but it will not come near you."

"If you say, 'The LORD is my refuge,' and you make the Most High your dwelling, no harm will overtake you, no disaster will come near your [home]. For he will command his angels concerning you to guard you in all your ways."

I wrote the Psalm out, inserting my name, and taped it over my bed.

"Because Bridget loves me," says the LORD, "I will rescue her. I will protect her … I will be with her in trouble, I will deliver her … With long life I will satisfy Bridget and show her my salvation."

Psalm 91 strengthened me through two surgeries and convalescences. *God, please don't let me die after losing my mom and getting married and having a son.* I figured, if God's in the business of life, I needed to trust him with mine.

The story of Jacob wrestling with an angel in Genesis 32 also gave me great comfort. In the narrative, Jacob met a stranger when he was all alone. They wrestled all night, and at dawn, the stranger asked Jacob to release him.

"Not until you bless me," Jacob replied. The stranger complied, and after he'd departed, Jacob realized he'd wrestled with God *and* gained God's approval for his tenacity.

My spirit, soul and body reached out and wrestled with God, for me to live and not die. For Bill and me to raise the son God had given us *together*. To be a physical manifestation of God's goodness in *life* rather than death.

In November of 2013, we finalized our adoption of Matthew. Four months later, I completed my final chemo treatment. Matthew did not lose another mother. I survived chemo and looked forward to what I dearly hoped would be a long life.

కాకాక

In 2012, Teresa Wright approached me as I worked in the nursery at Real Life.

"I just finished a book on forgiveness," she said. "It was very powerful. I think people need to know the power of forgiveness, so I'm going to teach a class on it here at the church. Would you be interested?"

"Yes, I would." I trusted Teresa and felt comfortable enough around her to reveal some of my own issues. "It's probably time for me to forgive my dad for all the crap he put my family through."

"Probably is," she said, laughing.

Do I really want to put myself in this position? I wondered as I approached the classroom door. *How will people feel about me if they know my true feelings toward Dad?*

I entered the room and looked around in amazement. People I knew at Real Life, who always looked like they had their act together, sat in a semi-circle. *These people have issues? They have stuff to deal with?*

As we worked through the course, person after person opened up about issues in their lives, people who'd greatly wronged them and how hard they struggled to forgive that person.

We also learned that forgiving a person didn't mean we had to maintain a close relationship with them — particularly those who'd abused us. Forgiveness sets us free from bitterness and sets our abusers free to find God's mercy if they choose.

I felt like I was on a roller coaster that whole year. I'd be going up-up-up basking in God's love and forgiveness for *me* and then down-down-down as I rehashed the gross wrongs done to my mom and me.

Dad took us to church as children, because it helped his image. He yelled at us all the way there. As soon as we pulled into the parking lot, Dad's demeanor changed. He became the essence of a loving husband and father.

We all followed his lead, putting on our own happy faces to the folks at church.

The moment we pulled away from the church, Dad resumed his true self and returned to the angry lecture our Sunday obligation had interrupted.

I remembered his constant ridicule and harshness toward all of us and his abandonment of me when I moved to Texas for a year. I remembered how hard Mom struggled financially while he lived in a nice home and enjoyed a good income.

If you don't forgive, I can't forgive you, I felt God trying to tell me.

"But, God, it's so *hard.*"

What makes your sin less sinful than his?

I struggled and fought, reasoned and argued. I wanted to yield to God, but unresolved pain blocked the way.

"If anyone would like to have prayer today, come up now," Andy said as he closed his message one Sunday.

Tears splashed down my cheeks as I walked to the front and bowed my head. "I have to let this go, God. I have to. The old memories pop up and haunt me. They poison my spirit and kill my joy. I want to be done with this, once and for all." I sank to my knees.

"At this moment, I *choose* to forgive Dad for every harsh word, cruel act and careless attitude toward Mom and us kids and all our struggles. I choose to put Dad's life in your hands and let you love him as hard as you love me. I choose to release every rotten grudge I've held against him, legitimate or not." I felt the heavy burden of unforgiveness lift from my tired shoulders and melt into the ground. "I choose to let go and let God."

శుశుశు

In late October 2014, Emily handed me a paper. "Would you do this?" she asked. "Would you be willing to tell your story for the book we are putting together here at Real Life?"

"I'll think about it."

"How can I do this, God?" I prayed as I listened to Bill and Matthew playing in the other room. "I killed a baby. I have no right to this joy."

You have to do this, I heard God say deep in my being. *You must let your own past go, and forgive yourself for your own sin. I already have, and you have no right to hang on to what I've forgiven. You need to tell your story for other women so that when they read it, they will not remain in the bondage as long as you have. Do it for them, Bridget.*

"You will have to give me the strength."

Of course. "My grace is sufficient for you, for my strength is made perfect in weakness."

"Okay, God. I trust you. I will do it."

Conclusion

My heart is full. When I became a pastor, my desire was to see people who'd been far away from God be raised to new life in Christ, to see people encouraged and the hurting and broken filled with hope. To be completely honest with you, as I have read these incredible stories, I saw that my dream of changed lives has been fulfilled! But the dream is not yet complete. At Real Life Church, we see the incredible things God has done — in the stories you've just read and in so many more lives — and believe it's just the beginning!

Every single time we see another changed life, another heart filled with hope, another future rising from the ashes of the past, it proves again how much God really loves people and that he is actively seeking to change lives. Think for just a moment: How did you get this book? And why you? We believe you read this book because God brought it to you seeking to reveal his love to you. It doesn't matter if you're a man or a woman, working on the assembly line or waiting tables, white collar, blue collar or no collar, a parent or a student, wealthy or poor. It doesn't matter what last name you were born with, how much money is in your bank account or what kind of trouble has filled your past, you NEED to KNOW that God loves you so much that he sent his son, Jesus, to SAVE YOU. He died so we could truly live. Jesus came to save all of us from the hellish pain of this world we've wallowed in and offer real peace, real joy and the opportunity to share in real life that will last forever through faith in Jesus Christ.

Do you have honest questions that such radical change is possible? It seems surreal, right? Too good to be true? On behalf of all of us at Real Life Church, I want to warmly invite you to come and check out our church family. Freely ask questions, examine our statements, see if we're "for real" and, if you choose, journey with us at whatever pace you are comfortable.

You will find that we are far from perfect. Our scars and wounds are still healing, and God is still completing the process of authentic life change in us. We still make mistakes in our journey — everyone will. We acknowledge our continued need for each other's forgiveness and support. We need the love of God just as much as we did the day before we believed in him.

We believe Real Life Church is a great place to encounter God and the plan he has for your life and journey in your relationship with him. Because we can't wait to meet you, we have prepared a special Web site portal for you to connect with us, learn more about God's plan for your life, receive prayer and learn about our church and what you can expect when you visit.

We encourage you to visit our Web site at www.RealLifeChurch.me.

Click on the "I've Read The Book" button, or simply go directly to www.RealLifeChurch.me/book. Let us know you've read the book, ask any questions and let us know how we can pray for you!

We really look forward to having you as a guest at Real Life Church. If you are unable to visit us, yet you intuitively sense you would like to experience a life change, then I encourage you to pray the prayer I will share with you at the end of this conclusion. Know that if your prayer genuinely comes from your heart, you will experience the beginning stages of authentic life change, similar to those you have read about.

How does this change occur?

Trust God with your future. Recognize that what you're doing isn't working. Accept the fact that God desires to forgive you and Jesus already paid the price for you to be forgiven for every bad decision, selfish motive and everything you have done to harm yourself or other people or to reject God. Realize that without this forgiveness, you will continue a life apart from God and his amazing love. In fact, in the Bible, the book of Romans, chapter 6, verse 23 tells us that the result of sin (seeking our way rather than God's way) is death, but the gift that God freely gives is everlasting life found in Jesus Christ. Choose to trust God with your future.

Trust God with your heart. There are things we all hold onto — hurts, broken dreams, pain and doubt. Many of these things become what defines us — certainly the things that have been done to us and even the things we have done to others. They become, at least in our minds, who we are. A victim of abuse, an unwanted child, a disability, a broken home, a drug addiction — fill in any part of your own story. Some would say that is who you are or at least what you have become. What you need to understand is that your past does not have to dictate your future. When you choose to trust God with your future, no longer does your past translate into your todays and tomorrows. Rather, what God says about your future affects change and allows you to live the Real Life you were created for. Trust God with all your heart. God passionately loves you and wants to give you a new heart. Ezekiel 11:19 reads, "I will give them singleness of heart and put a new spirit within them. I will take away their stony, stubborn heart and give them a tender, responsive heart" (NLT).

The Bible teaches us that "if you confess with your mouth that Jesus is Lord and believe in your heart that God raised him from the dead, you will be saved" (Romans 10:9 NLT).

Believe in your heart that because Jesus paid for your failure and wrong motives, and because you asked him to forgive you, he has filled your new heart with his life in such a way that he transforms you from the inside out. Second Corinthians 5:17 reads, "When someone becomes a Christian, he becomes a brand new person inside. He is not the same anymore. A new life has begun!"

Conclusion

Why not pray now?

Lord Jesus, I need you, and I am asking you to reveal yourself to me. I know now that I need to trust you with my whole life. My choices have not resulted in the happiness I hoped they would bring. Not only have I experienced pain, I've also caused it. I know I am separated from you, but I want that to change. I am sorry for the choices I've made that have hurt myself, hurt others and denied you. I believe your death paid for my sins and that you are now alive to change me from the inside out. Would you please do that in me now? I ask you to come and live in me so that I can sense you are here with me. Thank you for hearing and changing me. Now please help me know when you are speaking to me, so I can cooperate with your efforts to change me. Amen.

Mid-Michigan's unfolding story of God's love is still being written, and your name is in it. I hope to see you this Sunday!

Andy Shaver
Real Life Church
Charlotte, Michigan

We would love for you to join us at
Real Life Church!

Check out our Sunday morning service times at our
Web site: www.RealLifeChurch.me.

Our address is:
228 S. Cochran Avenue, Charlotte, MI 48813

Please call us at 517.541.5433 for directions,
or contact us at www.RealLifeChurch.me.

For more information on reaching your city with
stories from your church, go to
www.testimonybooks.com.

GOOD CATCH
PUBLISHING